"If this is your issue (and I suspect it is, given that you've picked up this book), then this is the place to start for clear, helpful, practical, gospel-motivated wisdom. It's goir ̣ ̣ be what we use with the guys at my chu ̣ ̣ struggle to get to grips wit ̣ ̣
Richard Perkins, Senior I ̣ London and Director of th ̣ Men's Convention committi

"Here is a timely, punchy bo ̣ , ̣ ̣ ̣ed with biblical truth, that will give fresh hope to the significant number of Christian men who have lost their assurance, usefulness and joy through a lack of self-control."
Paul Rees, Senior Pastor at Charlotte Chapel, Edinburgh

"All of us men struggle with self-control; and we seem to struggle with losing it in many of the same areas. This book reminds us that self-control is not only a gospel project, it is a church-wide project in which we all must play a part. So, if your desire is to struggle less and look like Jesus more, then you'll want to gather your friends and read this book together."
Juan R. Sanchez Jr, Senior Pastor, High Pointe Baptist Church, Austin, Texas, USA; Gospel Coalition Council member

"*A Man's Greatest Challenge* is no silver bullet when it comes to temptation and self-control. But neither should it be. Our help comes not from man's wisdom or experience, but from the Lord Jesus Christ. Dai Hankey points us very clearly to this powerful gospel. No silver bullet—but genuine hope for changed lives."
Dave McDonald, Senior Pastor at Stromlo Christian Church, Canberra, Australia, and Chaplain to ACT Brumbies; author of "Hope Beyond Cure"

"The smouldering ruins of a great city, walls breached and overthrown, is how the Bible pictures a life without self-control. Using this biblical picture, *A Man's Greatest Challenge* speaks Christ-centred challenge and hope into lives wrecked by a lack of self-control. This is an issue I face, as do my friends and church family. The combination of close biblical study and Dai's frank honesty makes this book that is both biblical and useful—a real-world guidebook full of grace and hope.

John Hindley, Pastor of BroadGrace, Norfolk, UK; author of "Serving without Sinking" and "You Can Really Grow"

"Men, read this book! In tackling the challenge of self-control, Dai shows that lasting hope lies not in will power but gospel power—its comfort and its call."

Gavin Peacock, Missions Pastor at Calvary Grace Church, Canada; former Chelsea and Newcastle midfielder

"Dai has done it again—managed to write a book that is both simple and hard to read ! Simple, because it is not long or complex; hard, because it is challenging to download into our lives. But that's a mark of a good book. It will help to identify your flaws and weaknesses, and discover a Christ-shaped, grace-filled response which leads to self-control."

Peter Baker, Senior Pastor at Lansdowne Baptist Church, Bournemouth, UK

"Dai Hankey has written an extremely helpful book for men and their struggles. Focussing on the core issue of self-control, this book has the capacity to set a man free from nagging sin and shame. I would recommend it as a book to be read by all—from teen through to senior."

Jamie Rasmussen, Senior Pastor, Scottsdale Bible Church, Arizona

A man's greatest challenge

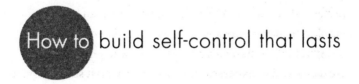

How to build self-control that lasts

Dai Hankey

To Andrew Rees, Nick Davis,
Chris Street and Peter Baker.

*You guys have helped me get a grip on my lifestyle,
marriage, ministry, testosterone, temper, family and
finances, and I am beyond grateful.*

A man's greatest challenge: *How to build self-control that lasts*
©Dai Hankey/The Good Book Company, 2014.

Published by
The Good Book Company
Tel (UK): 0333 123 0880
International: +44 (0) 208 942 0880
Email: info@thegoodbook.co.uk

Websites:
UK: www.thegoodbook.co.uk
North America: www.thegoodbook.com
Australia: www.thegoodbook.com.au
New Zealand: www.thegoodbook.co.nz

Unless otherwise indicated, Scripture quotations are from The Holy Bible,
English Standard Version (ESV), copyright © 2001 by Crossway, a publishing
ministry of Good News Publishers. Used by permission. All rights reserved.

ISBN: 9781909919860

Printed in the UK
Design by André Parker

Contents

1. Introduction

Have you ever done something for someone else, only to discover that in the process you got more out of it than they did?

That's pretty much the story of this book. What began as the discovery of a single Bible verse that I thought might be helpful for men who struggle with self-control went on to become a book-writing adventure that has, quite literally, changed my life. I am not the man I was when I first sat down to write this.

That might sound extreme, but it's true.

The battle for self-control has been the greatest challenge of my life. The faces of the issues I have sought to gain control over may have changed over the years, but the roots have remained and the struggle has never subsided. Looking back, my deepest regrets have come from losing control in one way or another. And my greatest frustrations have come from believing that I'd finally conquered certain sins, only to find my self-control failing as I messed up once again.

Perhaps now would be a good time for me to lay my cards on the table—to lift the mask of the man who is speaking to you. At the end of each of the chapters, you'll hear from different guys telling their stories of self-control struggles (and I want to thank them here for their courage and humility in sharing them).

Well, here's some of my story. I am a man who, at various stages in my life, has been wickedly and wildly out of control:

- I have deprived my family of hours of attention and affection, due to my inability to peel myself away from my smartphone.

- I have been that driver slamming his horn, cussing out other road users who dare to get in my way (if it was you, I'm sorry!)

- I have been the guy sitting in front of a screen, seduced and enslaved by lust and seemingly powerless to hit the "Off" button, as gratuitous sex scenes inflicted grievous damage upon my psyche and my soul.

- I have smashed up, torn down and punched through more things in fits of rage than I dare to remember.

However, I am writing this as a man who is now in control. The truths I have grappled with and the grace I have received in the process of writing this book have been truly transforming, both for myself and for those around me. Don't get me wrong—I am still very much a work in progress. I am not immune from losing control, and I stand in as much need of grace as I ever did. But I have found myself changed. I am no longer mastered by impulses that I cannot control. I am no longer a slave to my sin. I have found fulfilment and freedom—and self-control—in the gospel of Jesus.

I don't know you, and I don't know why you've decided to read this book (or, at least, to give the Introduction a go). But I do have a hunch that your greatest challenge, in one way or another, is to have self-control. And I'm guessing that you've found yourself thinking:

"I mustn't do that again. Right, I'm deciding: I won't do that again."

"Aaargh, I can't believe I just did it again. I hate feeling like this. OK, that's it. No more."

"It's been weeks now. This is going well. I've got this area sorted."

"I can't believe it. How can I have done it again?"

This book is about self-control: wanting it, and building it. But crucially, it's about self-control that *lasts*. That works. That changes your life, and changes the lives of those closest to you.

I want to tell you that building a life of lasting self-control is possible, though it is a challenge that requires honesty, sweat, tears, humility and faith. I'm praying that the gospel truths in this book would change your life as you read it as much as they have changed mine as I've written it.

2. Damage

The second instalment of *The Lord of the Rings* reaches a thrilling climax as a mob of snarling, heavily armed, bloodthirsty Uruk-hai (the bad guys) rock up to Helm's Deep, the citadel of the Rohirrim (the good guys).

As strongholds go, Helm's Deep is as formidable as they come, its vast walls providing a seemingly impenetrable defence against invading armies.

Saruman, the Commander-in-Chief of the Uruk-hai, knows the challenge is simple:

"If the wall is breached, Helm's Deep will fall."

The wall is all that matters. The wall is all that stands between the people of Rohan and certain defeat.

And how right Saruman proves to be. The walls are impregnably strong. Helm's Deep appears safe. Until a flame-wielding Uruk exploits the only weakspot in Helm's Deep's defences—a drain underneath the wall. He detonates a cauldron of gunpowder in that part of the wall, and his comrades pour through the resulting gaping hole to pillage, plunder and put the city to the sword.

The wall is breached. Helm's Deep falls. The town is destroyed.

Walls matter. And they don't just matter in the fantasy land of Middle Earth. In the real ancient world, walls mattered. They were the primary means of defence. A city that was surrounded by towering walls was a daunting proposition for invading armies. Towers high up in the walls provided watchmen with a vantage point from which they could spot approaching danger and muster the troops to arms. Walls gave archers and defending soldiers a strategically elevated position from which to repel enemy forces.

Walls were how you kept the bad guys out. The stronger your walls, the more secure and peaceful and prosperous your city.

But, if the walls were breached, the city was as good as taken.

The ruined city

So picture the city whose walls have been breached, a city now lying in smouldering ruins.

Its once proud walls, now reduced to rubble and ash, testify to defeat and defencelessness. Life in the city is no longer prosperous and joy-filled. Faith, hope and love have been plundered. Streets once energised by song and laughter now broadcast the tragic lament of loss and grief. Peace has been replaced with anxiety. Shame and fear lurk in the shadows.

Picture that scene, and then read this amazing proverb, written by King Solomon 3,000 years ago:

> Like a city whose walls are broken down is a man who lacks
> self-control.   (Proverbs 25 v 28, NIV1984 translation)

You and I are mini-cities. And we need walls to protect us; not walls built out of bricks and mortar, but self-control.

Because, make no mistake, if you are a Christian, you are a man under attack. Whether you like it or not, the devil wants to take you down. He wants to destroy your life and ultimately your faith. Every day, we face "the schemes of the devil. For we do not wrestle against flesh and blood, but ... against the spiritual forces of evil" (Ephesians 6 v 16).

Every day, Satan launches temptation after temptation at you. And what is your protection? Your self-control. Your ability to say "no" when that's necessary; to hold your tongue when you need to; to step back when that's best, and step up when you're called to.

Your greatest challenge

I don't think most of us think very much, talk very much or pray very much about self-control. But our self-control is all that stands between us and devastation. It's what makes the difference between a life of security and contentment, and an existence of vulnerability and regret.

And so self-control is every man's greatest challenge. When we don't build our wall, when we are weak, the consequences are devastating.

Take a moment to consider which areas of your life are most prone to lacking self-control, so that when temptations come, the wall is breached.

Any time you have thought: "I wish I hadn't done/said/ thought that", chances are you lacked self-control.

For many of us the area of greatest concern is sex—we are simply unable to break free of the grip that lust, pornography, masturbation and fornication have on our lives. For others it may be an explosive temper coupled with a short fuse. Some of us are literally ruled by our technology or serve as slaves to social media, while for others the issue is materialism and money. Some struggle to strike a healthy balance between work and family life. Others might be addicted to drugs or alcohol, while still others simply can't keep our words, thoughts or emotions in check. It may simply be an inability to be polite to other drivers when you're behind the wheel; or to stop your hand stretching out to take the third helping of food.

You might be someone who is completely out of control. You have no walls at all. The devil can attack you at virtually any point and you're defeated. But you might be someone who is self-controlled in virtually every area... except one, or two. And the devil will attack you at that point, just as that Uruk-hai found the drain, the one point of weakness at Helm's Deep. At that point, the strength elsewhere in your life doesn't matter at all. A single area of weakness in your self-control leaves you prone to defeat.

And the implications of living as a man who has not built self-control are potentially ruinous. Not just for you, but for those you live and work and spend time with. Sooner or later, there is always someone on the receiving end of our lust, rage, laziness, and addiction... and it's often those who are closest to us.

Think about the last time you messed up due to a lack of self-control.

- Who got hurt? Who will get hurt in the future if it's a habitual pattern of behaviour in you?

- What got spoiled?

- How did you end up worrying about what would happen next?

Brothers, if only we had self-control! Self-control would allow us to be the men God wants us to be. The men we, deep down, long to be. The men those close to us need us to be.

So let me encourage you, at the start of this book, to read it prayerfully. Ask the Holy Spirit to search you, enable you to spot any excuses you're making, help you see how and where the Bible is speaking to your life, and change you more and more into that strong, secure, resilient, dependable man you would love to be.

Learning from kings

Now I appreciate that "walls during the time of the Old Testament kings" might not be the sort of thing you'd ordinarily talk about with your mates over a drink, but I have to confess that I'm gripped by it. Allow me to elaborate...

Basically, when a God-fearing king was on the throne, statues of fake gods—idols—were torn down, and the walls of the nation's towns were built. Security was maintained and the people enjoyed times of peace, prosperity and blessing. The reign of King Asa is a great example of this:

> And Asa did what was good and right in the eyes of the
> LORD his God. He took away the foreign altars and the high
> places and broke down the pillars and cut down the Asherim
> and commanded Judah to seek the LORD, the God of their
> fathers, and to keep the law and the commandment. He also
> took out of all the cities of Judah the high places and the
> incense altars. And the kingdom had rest under him. He
> built fortified cities in Judah, for the land had rest. He had
> no war in those years, for the Lord gave him peace. And he
> said to Judah, "Let us build these cities and surround them

with walls and towers, gates and bars. The land is still ours, because we have sought the LORD our God. We have sought him, and he has given us peace on every side." So they built and prospered.   (2 Chronicles 14 v 1-7)

When an ungodly king was in power, the opposite happened. Idol-shrines were built; the city wall-building budget was under-funded. And so, in God's judgment, the untended city walls would be breached, and cities plundered and destroyed. Perhaps the most devastating account of this is found in 2 Chronicles 36 v 17-19:

Therefore [God] brought up against them the king of the Chaldeans, who killed their young men with the sword in the house of their sanctuary and had no compassion on young man or virgin, old man or aged. He gave them all into his hand. And all the vessels of the house of God, great and small, and the treasures of the house of the LORD, and the treasures of the king and of his princes, all these he brought to Babylon. And they burned the house of God and broke down the wall of Jerusalem and burned all its palaces with fire and destroyed all its precious vessels.

Let's apply this to ourselves. The godly man will identify, and deal with, the idols in his life. And he'll work on building up his walls—which, Solomon tells us, means building self-control. The result? Security, peace, rest, etc.

But equally, we can live the opposite way. We can worship our idols, building for things that we love more than God. We can live without self-control. And we will face disaster: a disaster that we may blame on everything and everyone but ourselves, but that truthfully is down to our misjudged building priorities.

You may not be an Old Testament king. But you are a man who will either build his walls, or won't. Which will it be?

The king who changed his mind

An interesting Old Testament king to throw into the mix at this point is Manasseh. Manasseh started off as a thoroughly nasty piece of work—worshipping the stars, burning his kids, promoting idolatry in the temple of God. Morally and spiritually, he was spiralling out of control and leading the entire nation down the same dark path:

> Manasseh ... did what was evil in the sight of the LORD ...
> For he rebuilt the high places [places where people went to
> worship idols] that his father Hezekiah had broken down,
> and he erected altars to the Baals, and made Asherahs, and
> worshipped all the host of heaven and served them. And
> he built altars in the house of the LORD, of which the LORD
> had said, "In Jerusalem shall my name be for ever." And he
> built altars for all the host of heaven in the two courts of the
> house of the LORD. And he burned his sons as an offering in
> the Valley of the Son of Hinnom, and used fortune-telling
> and omens and sorcery, and dealt with mediums and with
> wizards. He did much evil in the sight of the LORD, provoking
> him to anger. And the carved image of the idol that he had
> made he set in the house of God ... Manasseh led Judah and
> the inhabitants of Jerusalem astray, to do more evil than the
> nations whom the LORD destroyed before the people of Israel.
> (2 Chronicles 33 v 1-9)

You can guess what happened next:

> The LORD spoke to Manasseh and to his people, but they
> paid no attention. Therefore the LORD brought upon them
> the commanders of the army of the king of Assyria, who
> captured Manasseh with hooks and bound him with chains
> of bronze and brought him to Babylon. (v 10-11)

As Manasseh floundered in a Babylonian jail, he had time and space to reflect on his reckless, rebellious life and, as he did so, something incredible happened. He cried out to God for mercy:

> And when he was in distress, he entreated the favour of the
> LORD his God and humbled himself greatly before the God of his
> fathers. He prayed to him, and God was moved by his entreaty
> and heard his plea and brought him again to Jerusalem into his
> kingdom. Then Manasseh knew that the LORD was God. (v 12-13)

Mannaseh was a changed man. He became a godly king. And godly kings build the walls and destroy the idols:

> Afterwards he built an outer wall for the city of David west
> of Gihon, in the valley, and for the entrance into the Fish
> Gate, and carried it around Ophel, and raised it to a very great
> height. He also put commanders of the army in all the fortified
> cities in Judah. And he took away the foreign gods and the idol
> from the house of the LORD, and all the altars that he had built
> on the mountain of the house of the LORD and in Jerusalem,
> and he threw them outside the city. He also restored the altar
> of the LORD and offered on it sacrifices of peace offerings and
> of thanksgiving, and he commanded Judah to serve the LORD,
> the God of Israel. (2 Chronicles 33 v 14-16)

Mannaseh shows that it is possible to change, and that it is necessary to change. You can change. You need to.

Three kinds of men

This book is written for three kinds of men.

1. Early Manasseh (Rebellious)

You enjoy all that life has given you, with yourself at the centre of your life. Whatever feels good, is good. You worship what you think will make you happy and fulfilled, and you can't really name a way you've been tempted recently—because you give in to each temptation before recognising it. To be honest, self-control sounds like a one-way ticket to a boring, colourless life; you're not quite sure why you're even reading this. And here's the thing: you could be early Manasseh while looking like a Christian, or even while being in church leadership. After all, Manasseh was king of God's people. Don't assume this type of man isn't you just because you're in church on Sunday mornings with your game face on. What does the rest of your life look like?

Are you this man?

2. Mid-story Manasseh (Wrecked)

You may be more like Manasseh at his lowest ebb. A man at rock bottom, shackled by the shame of sinful behaviour, addiction and weakness. There are no excuses left to make. You are all too aware that your failure to build self-control into your life has left you defeated and destitute. You can see, when you dare to look, the devastating impact your lack of control has had on those you love. Self-control sounds impossible.

Are you this man?

3. Later Manasseh (Repentant)

Finally, perhaps you are more like Manasseh after God has finally won his heart. A man who has cried out to God from the depths of disgrace and has mercifully encountered his grace. A man who has gratefully grabbed forgiveness and a fresh start with both hands, and is now passionately committed to rebuilding the walls and regaining control of his life. A man of courageous repentance. You know there are weakpoints in your walls. You want to build them strong.

Are you this man?

Whoever you are, let the story of Manasseh give you hope. Whatever has happened, you are not further gone than he was. You are not beyond repair. Equally, whoever you are, you are not without need of repair.

It will be no small task. It's going to be a long, costly and all-consuming building project, but it's going to be worth it to become a godly, self-controlled man / disciple / husband / dad / churchman / colleague / friend / neighbour (delete as appropriate).

You can be a city with walls.

Before we get building, however, we need to discover what a life of self-control actually looks like...

Craig's story

Like most teenagers I discovered alcohol, but as I got older, I came to depend on it more and more. At first, I drank because it was a quick and easy way to feel good.

My philosophy was: do whatever feels good now, and worry about the consequences later! What I wanted to do was drink, so I did—more and more. Through my twenties my life gradually crumbled around me, and I dragged a lot of people into the pit that I was digging. By the time I was in my early thirties, I was jobless, friendless, broke, living in my mother's house and spending my benefits on getting as hammered as I could as often as I could. Day after day I sat on the floor in my bedroom drinking until I passed out, then waking up and starting to drink again. I lied constantly, I pushed people away, and I hurt all those who loved me but were powerless to help. My life had become nothing but pain and misery to me and my family. But I couldn't really see it.

Amazingly, despite a lifelong commitment to atheism, I was suddenly and unexpectedly saved three years ago. The transformation since then has been unbelievable. Not only am I completely free of addiction, but God has given me a job, a home and a wonderful, godly wife.

Before I was saved, I just saw life as one self-centred step after another towards nowhere in particular, and so I had no desire to discipline myself because I had no goal. Now I know that the greatest goal in life is knowing Christ, and the best way to achieve that is step after step, a day at a time, but always with my eyes on the ultimate prize.

Juan's story

I'm a Christian, a husband and a father, and an active member of my church. I think that from the outside I probably don't look like a guy who struggles with self-control.

And I don't, at least not in the obvious ways like drugs and adultery. But I've come to realise that my thoughts are often a long way from my control. And the way it shows itself is that I find it almost impossible to switch off from work. I get home, and I'm with my family, but in my spare moments I'm thinking about a project, or a conversation at the office, or a meeting the next day.

I guess some would say I sound conscientious. But in fact, it means that when I'm with my family, I'm not really all there for them. My lack of self-control means that they miss out on my full focus. I'll check my smartphone for work emails while I'm meant to be playing with my young children. I won't really engage with my wife because I'm musing on a work issue. And I will find my thoughts wandering while I'm praying.

Thankfully, God has enabled me to see that, if unchecked, this area of weakness could cause some real damage to my faith and to the way I act with my family, and give me some real re-grets when I look back. To fix a problem, you first have to spot that it's a problem; and though I haven't gained self-control in this area all the time, I am at the stage of noticing when it's happening, and beginning to deal with it moment by moment. By God's grace, I'll become more the husband and father my family want me to be. No one outside will really notice, I im-agine—it's not like I'm stopping an affair or giving up getting drunk—but my family will feel the benefit.

3. Blueprint

I love it when a plan comes together!

John "Hannibal" Smith

Lessons in Lego

Boys love playing with Lego. At least, my two sons do.

But they don't all play with it in the same way, as I have learned from watching my two wonderfully different boys.

Take my eldest son, Josiah. When he is given a new Lego set, we know exactly what to expect. He opens the box with surgical precision and tips the pieces into a neat pile on the table. Then he sits there for hours, diligently following the instructions to the letter until, brick by brick, the building is complete. The finished product always looks exactly like it does on the box—not a piece out of place. Perfect!

Josiah's younger brother, Ezra, takes a very different approach! While his big brother is busy building at the table, Ezra will be sat on the floor, tipping bricks over his head or scattering them in a million different directions. The instruction booklet hasn't been seen for some time, not that it's ever been missed. The two minutes that Ezra might dedicate to the project generally consist of him smashing random bricks together with passionate determination, but zero care or attention. When he's done, his project will invariably look like a scene from a disaster movie.

Basically, I am father to Bob the Builder and Demolition Man!

Christ our blueprint

As we consider the daunting challenge of rebuilding walls and fortifying our lives with self-control, it might be worth thinking about my boys and their Lego. If, like Josiah, we're going to construct something sturdy and strong, we certainly need patience. But we also need a plan—a clear idea of what exactly it is that we are seeking to build. So...

What does a man with walls of self-control actually look like?

Josiah has a picture on the front of a box to aim for, but what do we get?

We don't get to look at a picture on a box; we get to look at a man in history. A life has been lived that was supremely, perfectly, beautifully self-controlled. Self-control has been modelled for us by Jesus Christ. It's worth reading through a Gospel account of his life with this theme of self-control in your mind, and just seeing this amazing portrait of a man with impenetrable walls of control. The Gospels provide us with, if you like, the picture on the Lego box—the Lord Jesus.

So, for example, here are a few compelling examples from the Gospel of Matthew that show us what Jesus-style self-control looks like.

Temptation under control

Before commencing his ministry, Jesus was led into the wilderness by the Holy Spirit, where he was tested, tried and tempted by the devil. And Jesus stood up to everything that Satan threw at him.

After 40 days of prayer and fasting, the battle reached its climax:

> Then Jesus was led up by the Spirit into the wilderness to be
> tempted by the devil. And after fasting forty days and forty
> nights, he was hungry. And the tempter came and said to
> him, "If you are the Son of God, command these stones to
> become loaves of bread."   (Matthew 4 v 1-3)

Jesus was hungry. He could use his power to tend to his own needs so easily. How attractive. How tempting. Would his wall be breached?

> But he answered, "It is written,
> 'Man shall not live by bread alone,
>   but by every word that comes from the mouth of God.'" (v 4)

No! So Satan tried a different part of the wall:

> Then the devil took him to the holy city and set him on the
> pinnacle of the temple and said to him, "If you are the Son of
> God, throw yourself down, for it is written,
>
> 'He will command his angels concerning you',
>
> and
>
> 'On their hands they will bear you up,
>   lest you strike your foot against a stone.'" (v 5-6)

Jesus had a whole ministry ahead of him. He could use his power to respond to the devil's teasing "*If* you are..." by proving himself. How obvious. How tempting. Would his wall be breached ?

> Jesus said to him, "Again it is written, 'You shall not put the
> Lord your God to the test.'" (v 7)

No! And now came the third wave of attack:

> Again, the devil took him to a very high mountain and
> showed him all the kingdoms of the world and their glory.
> And he said to him, "All these I will give you, if you will fall
> down and worship me." (v 8-9)

Jesus' path to glory lay through death on a cross. He knew that. But it didn't have to—the devil offered him every glory the world can offer, just for the price of bending his knee to the devil. Jesus could avoid torture and execution! He could have it all without the rejection and the suffering! How tempting. Would his wall be breached?

> Then Jesus said to him, "Be gone, Satan! For it is written,
>   'You shall worship the Lord your God
>   and him only shall you serve.'"
> Then the devil left him... (v 10-11)

Jesus saw temptation for what it was. And he met it with iron self-control. What really strikes me about this showdown is the timing of it—it all happened when Jesus was tired and alone. Is there a man on earth who doesn't struggle to exercise self-control when he is tired, hungry and alone? If there is, I certainly haven't met him! But Jesus stayed focused, clung to Scripture, stood his ground... and "the devil left him", beaten back by the walls.

Don't you wish that you were that strong in the face of temptation? That after an exhausting day at work... or when your wife and kids are fast asleep in bed... or while away on that business trip... the porn site, the minibar or the flirtatious colleague were simply unable to breach your defences?

That's the kind of man that I want to be.

What about you?

Fear under control

As the shadow of the cross loomed ever larger and the pressures intensified, Jesus' self-control became even more impressive. Here he is, the night before his death. Read this as a picture of a self-controlled man:

> Then Jesus went with them to a place called Gethsemane, and he said to his disciples, "Sit here, while I go over there and pray." And taking with him Peter and the two sons of Zebedee, he began to be sorrowful and troubled. Then he said to them, "My soul is very sorrowful, even to death; remain here, and watch with me." And going a little farther he fell on his face and prayed, saying, "My Father, if it be possible, let this cup pass from me; nevertheless, not as I will, but as you will." And he came to the disciples and found them sleeping. And he said to Peter, "So, could you not watch with me one hour? Watch and pray that you may not enter into temptation. The spirit indeed is willing, but the flesh is weak." Again, for the second time, he went away and prayed, "My Father, if this cannot pass unless I drink it, your will be done." And again he came and found them sleeping, for their eyes were heavy. So, leaving them again, he went away and prayed for the third time, saying the same words again. Then he came to the disciples and said to them, "Sleep and take your rest later on. See, the hour is at hand, and the Son of Man is betrayed into the hands of sinners. Rise, let us be going; see, my betrayer is at hand."   (Matthew 26 v 36-46)

As his weak-willed disciples slept, Jesus was left alone to contemplate the unspeakable agonies that lay ahead. Luke even records that his sweat turned to blood (Luke 22 v 44), such was the level of stress. Yet even in those darkest, most traumatic moments as Jesus wrestled with horror of what it would cost him to bear the full weight of God's wrath against sin, he didn't lose clarity, courage or control. He could have quit right there and then, but he chose instead to align himself with his Father's will and thus stayed on course for the cross.

Fear would have run from the situation. Fear would have shouted at the sleeping friends. Self-control walked towards the cross.

Imagine possessing such self-control that even when surrounded by failed relationships and confronted with unimaginable terrors, you were never at risk of throwing in the towel and walking away!

That's the kind of man that I want to be.

What about you?

Power under control

The strain on the Son of God at this moment was utterly relentless:

> While he was still speaking, Judas came, one of the twelve, and with him a great crowd with swords and clubs, from the chief priests and the elders of the people. Now the betrayer had given them a sign, saying, "The one I will kiss is the man; seize him." And he came up to Jesus at once and said, "Greetings, Rabbi!" And he kissed him. Jesus said to him, "Friend, do what you came to do." Then they came up and laid hands on Jesus and seized him. And behold, one of those who were with Jesus stretched out his hand and drew his sword and struck the servant of the high priest and cut off his ear. Then Jesus said to him, "Put your sword back into its place. For all who take the sword will perish by the sword. Do you think that I cannot appeal to my Father, and he will at once send me more than twelve legions of angels? But how

then should the Scriptures be fulfilled, that it must be so?"
At that hour Jesus said to the crowds, "Have you come out as
against a robber, with swords and clubs to capture me? Day
after day I sat in the temple teaching, and you did not seize
me. But all this has taken place that the Scriptures of the
prophets might be fulfilled." Then all the disciples left him
and fled.   (Matthew 26 v 47-56)

This encounter blows my mind! Betrayed by a close friend into
the clutches of a mob of hate-fuelled religious extremists, it's
amazing to think about what Jesus *didn't* do. He *didn't* opt for the
"lashing out" option (like Peter) or the "run away" option (as the
disciples all ended up doing). The most powerful person in this
scene was the one with twelve legions (that's around 64,800)
of angels at his disposal. It's Jesus. But he kept his power in
check. He would use his power for others, not for himself; his
plan was victory over sin on the cross, not an angelic victory over
his enemies on the hillside. So the angels stayed in heaven and
Jesus stayed on mission.

Just let that sink in for a moment. Jesus didn't shrink back, but
neither did he fight back. Rather, he dug deep and pressed on.
He had infinite power, under perfect control. What an example
for us men to follow! God has made us strong. What would it
look like for our families, our churches, our work places and
our communities if we had our strength under such control that
rather than being spineless or reckless, we would be irresistibly
courageous and faithful to the end.

That's the kind of man that I want to be.

What about you?

Tongue under control

Following his arrest, Jesus was dragged before the high priest. He was mocked, spat upon and then brought to the Roman governor, Pilate. As he stood before the man who had the power to condemn him to death, listening to the barrage of malicious lies and accusations made against him, Jesus once again demonstrated a whole other level of self-control. It came in the form of silence:

> Now Jesus stood before the governor, and the governor asked him, "Are you the King of the Jews?" Jesus said, "You have said so." But when he was accused by the chief priests and elders, he gave no answer. Then Pilate said to him, "Do you not hear how many things they testify against you?" But he gave him no answer, not even to a single charge, so that the governor was greatly amazed.   (Matthew 27 v 11-14)

That's staggering! In the face of such abuse, such injustice and such murderous conspiracy, Jesus didn't lose it! He didn't demand justice, self-justify, dish out threats or lay out his divine credentials. Rather, he kept his lips locked, proving himself to be unlike any other man who has ever lived—a man with a tamed tongue.

As soon as we learn to talk, we know what it's like to say something we wish later we hadn't. We know what it is to lose control of our tongue. Jesus never did that. *Never.*

How awesome would it be if we could control our tongues like that? Not entering into gossip about that really annoying colleague at work. Not having to delete that tweet or change that status that you posted in a moment of annoyance or rage. Not responding harshly to our wives and kids, even when they're wrong! Imagine being so full of grace and truth that nothing else ever came out of your mouth.

That's the kind of man that I want to be.

What about you?

Gospel ambition

These are just a few snapshots from the life of Christ; we could have considered plenty more. But... it's tempting at this point to try to find some gaps in Jesus' resumé:

"What about family? Jesus was never a dad, so what does he know about being pushed to the limit by sleepless babies, tantrum-throwing toddlers or hormone-crazed teenagers?"

"What about work? Jesus didn't have a proper job, so surely he can't relate to the demands of working a long day, the pressure of paying bills, or what it's like to have a boss who does none of the work and takes all of the praise?"

"What about... (insert your issue here)?"

In other words: *Jesus, if you faced what I face, you'd be a little less self-controlled.*

But in fact, there are no gaps in his resumé, as this little nugget from Hebrews 4 v 15 informs us:

For we do not have a high priest [ie: Jesus] who is unable to sympathize with our weaknesses, but one who in every respect has been tempted as we are, yet without sin.

Jesus knew what it was to be tired, disappointed, betrayed, pressured, criticised and unfairly accused. He knew it all because he experienced it first-hand as a man, just like us.

Do you really think that in your life you face temptations like the ones he did in the desert? That you confront fear as he did in Gethsemane? You think your life is harder than his? No, Jesus has been tempted just as you and I are—and yet at every moment and in every way, Jesus exercised epic self-control.

Thrillingly, that means that, as we look at this man, we see what it means to live with self-control. Challengingly, it means that, as men like him, we have no excuse for not living with self-control. He was a man just as we are; if he could do it, we should do it too. This man is our blueprint:

> By this we may know that we are in [Christ]: whoever says
> he abides in him ought to walk in the same way in which he
> walked. (1 John 2 v 5-6)

Re-read that. That is huge! If I call myself a Christian, I ought to live just as Jesus did. That's the standard. There's the blueprint. This verse is crucial in helping us truly to come to grips with the scale of this building project. The reason that it is so pivotal is that it refuses to let us proceed any further with small ambition and a limited mindset. If you have approached this book with the idea that what you would like is simply to gain a bit more control over your life, to curb your porn addiction, to get the discipline to diet, or to become a better man than you were before, then, in love, I want to suggest that you are setting your sights way too low.

You might be content with cobbling together a rickety garden fence, but God wants you to build massive city walls. He doesn't want you to improve; he wants you to be perfect! He doesn't want you to get a bit more self-controlled, but *completely* self-controlled.

Let's not settle for merely becoming better men. Our blueprint is to be like Jesus, and nothing less will do.

That's gospel ambition!

And I guess that's where this book will differ significantly from most other books on the subject of self-control. Rather than providing you with seven simple steps to gain control over your life, I am daring you to take up the challenge of seeking to become a man like Jesus. Does that sound like mission impossible to you?

Good. Because it is!

In fact there is more chance of Ezra building a Lego bridge to the moon and back than there is of you managing to live like Jesus; because there's not a man on the planet who is capable of pulling that off. We have all fallen miserably short of his standards and, despite our best efforts, we continue to do so.

So how can this blueprint ever become reality? Surely this project is doomed to fail from the start?! The man you want to be is a man you cannot be, right? Your walls of self-control could never be rebuilt to that perfect standard... could they?

Well... no... at least, not if we're the ones in charge. But "nothing is impossible with God" (Luke 1 v 37, NIV84). God is not calling you to do anything he is not equipping you to do.

Christ-like walls can be built, whoever you are and whatever your character and your past. And it starts with getting rid of the wreckage.

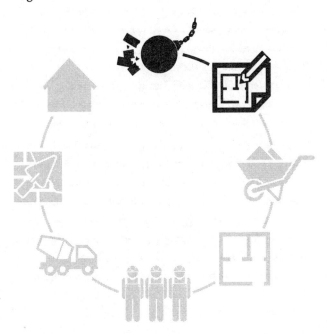

Sam's story

I guess like many of you who are reading this book, my most prevalent struggle as a young man in my teens was with lust. I was taken captive at the tender age of ten. This was a battle of monumental proportions that waged often unchecked for some twelve years.

But more recently I have had other areas where self-control has been wanting. I have been married now for three years and I often take my beautiful wife for granted. There are even times, I am ashamed to say, when I know I am acting in a way which is crushing her spiritual growth rather than encouraging it. What I am talking about are actions or words (or a lack of them) that ultimately centre on my wants and desires, rather than on hers.

But as I look into the Gospel accounts of the life of Jesus and I ponder his actions towards the social outcast, the prostitute and the betrayer, it is hard not to be ashamed at the way I treat the woman whom I love. At times I have even thought about denying Bec things she wants because we can't afford it, when in actual fact the reason we can't afford it is because I have prioritised something I want! Isn't it amazing that I struggle with self-control when it comes to loving the person I love most in this world—it shows just how selfish I am.

Sometimes I measure myself against others around me and then I can feel chuffed that I'm better than them. But when I look at Christ, I'm floored by seeing just how beautiful he was in having such control of himself that he was able to love others properly. But the great thing is that I can fix my eyes firmly on him, not only as the One who epitomises self-control, but also as the One who gives me the grace to model it. It's as I look at him that I can learn to be a better, more loving husband.

4. Clearance

More than once, I've wished my real life had a delete key.

Harlan Coben

Destruction

I was in the house getting my baby daughter dressed when all of a sudden there was a loud bang on the door. As I answered, I could see that the policeman on the other side had a very serious face. The reason rapidly became clear:

"Your row of houses is on fire and you need to evacuate now!"

Naturally, I took evasive action and legged it out of the house, dragging our confused dog with one hand and carrying my little girl in the other. The street was rammed with residents who were all gazing at the thick plume of black smoke billowing out of the roof of one of the houses just a few doors down. The firemen fought the flames long into the night, but by the time they eventually prevailed, three of the houses in our row had been destroyed.

I returned the next day to assess the damage. The houses that had caught alight were now just a smouldering wreck. The walls were gone. It was a scene of devastation.

A few days, later a security guard took up residence in a caravan next to the site. He told me that he had been employed to protect the properties from theft. I was stunned to learn that on the very same night that the fire had raged, thieves had broken in to steal whatever they could lay their hands on.

I guess that's what happens when walls are breached and burned.

The houses needed rebuilding from the ground up. However, before the builders could start, there was another job they had to do first.

They had to clear the wreckage.

Their team set to work piling charred wood, burnt furniture, smashed tiles and other such stuff into wheelbarrows, chucking it into skips and whisking it away. Weeks later, once all the rubble had finally been cleared away, there was a large, gaping gap in the middle of our terrace.

Only now could the building begin.

Go for the impossible

I share that story because it perfectly illustrates what this chapter is all about. We have seen that self-control is a challenge for us all, and that if we truly want to be men of self-control, our goal is to be like Jesus. Nothing else will do. We have also acknowledged that this is impossible apart from the grace and power of God in our lives.

Yet here you are in Chapter Four, which means that rather than letting pride, despair or despondency get the better of you, you've chosen instead to go for the impossible—to rebuild the walls.

And I am so glad you did, but here's my concern...

You might try to launch yourself into a spiritual construction project without first facing up to and clearing away the dirt and debris of past destruction. No builder in his right mind would mix cement and stack bricks on piles of charred rubble. In the same way, there may well be some wreckage in your life that you need to get rid of before the spade-and-trowel work can truly begin. Rather than simply trying to sweep the past under the carpet or attempting to move on in the grip of shame and regret, you need to clear all of that junk.

But how?

Well, Solomon might have got us started on this building project, but when it comes to learning how to deal with the mangled wreckage of a life that has spiralled wildly out of control, there's no one better to spend some time with than Solomon's dad, King David.

Number fifty-one

David did not only kill giants—he was also a prolific songwriter (about half the psalms are attributed to him). And one of King David's songs is a masterclass in dealing with the carnage of a reckless, wretched past.

Psalm 51 is written about the events recorded in 2 Samuel 11. I'd encourage you to go back and read the passage for yourself, but, in a nutshell, David sees a beautiful woman bathing herself, lacks the self-control to stop looking and lusting, and ends up inviting her to share his bed. Trouble is, this lady, Bathsheba, is another man's wife. And she gets pregnant; and since her husband, Uriah, is away fighting David's battles, there's only one man who can be the father. David ends up arranging Uriah's death to cover up his sin. His lack of self-control has destroyed a woman's purity and a man's existence.

And it cannot be covered up—not from God. In what must be one of the most terrifying missions anyone's been sent on, the prophet Nathan is sent by God to expose David's sin to him. Nathan had to say to David: *God hasn't bought the cover-up.*

And the way that David responded to the train-wreck he had caused is what we are focusing on in this chapter. Of all the psalms David wrote, without doubt the one that I have personally gone back to more often than any other is number 51.

Why? Because you could call it a step-by-step lesson in how to clear the wreckage out of your life.

Let's take a look.

Step one: GOD—turn to him

> Have mercy on me, O God,
> according to your steadfast love;
> according to your abundant mercy
> blot out my transgressions.
> Wash me thoroughly from my iniquity,
> and cleanse me from my sin! (Psalm 51 v 1-2)

Notice that right from the start, David acknowledges that he needs help—and that the help he needs can only come from God.

As men, we are so often unlike this. We all respond in different ways when we mess up, but chances are your response is one of the following:

- Self justification—I'm not that bad.
- Self deception—I didn't do it.
- Self help—I'll fix myself.
- Self hatred—I'm scum.
- Self pity—I'm a victim.

We locate the excuse or the solution in *self*. Which is great, except for one thing—none of it works. None of it clears the wreckage and allows us to move on and build again.

David doesn't choose any of those options. Rather, he focuses all his energy and attention on the only One who is capable of clearing up the collateral damage of sin, both within him and around him. He cries out to God.

And he cries out to him confidently.

> Have mercy on me ... according to your steadfast love;
> according to your abundant mercy. (v 1)

David knew that God's love is unshakable and that he never runs out of mercy, which is why, despite the horrific nature of his sin, he knew where to turn. I fear that many of us men are far more persuaded of our wretchedness than we are of God's love. While that remains the case, we will instinctively turn away from God in shame, rather than humbly turning to him for mercy. Conversely, the more aware we are of God's love, the quicker we will turn to him for help. We need to remember both the truth about ourselves—we're wretched—and the truth about God— he is abundantly merciful.

The first step to removing the wreckage of past shame is to turn to God.

The next step is to face the full horror of our mess.

Step two: GUILT—own it

"Hankey, Miss wants to see you now!" I could tell from the tone of my friend's voice that I was in trouble, and I knew exactly what for. A few hours previously I, along with some of my mates, had taken a marker pen and graffiti'ed pretty much every surface in

one of the school classrooms. What bothered me, however, was that I was the only one who was being summoned.

"What about the others?" I protested.

"You're the only one who wrote your name, you idiot!" came the crushing reply.

My first instinct was to blame others. My second was to protest my innocence; but I quickly realised that my name was, quite literally, all over the crime. I came clean.

David comes clean. He approaches God with raw honesty and says: "It was me. My name is all over this. I'm guilty as charged."

Here's how he puts it:

> For I know my transgressions, and my sin is ever before me.
> Against you, you only, have I sinned
> and done what is evil in your sight,
> so that you may be justified in your words
> and blameless in your judgment.
> Behold, I was brought forth in iniquity,
> and in sin did my mother conceive me. (v 3-5)

I'm so gripped by David's brutal honesty here. Here is the most powerful, the most famous and the most respected man in the kingdom, publicly facing up to the wreckage in his life. The language is strong and humbling. He doesn't blame adverse circumstances, a troubled past, a sexless marriage, a seductive temptress, or even God. He doesn't compare himself to others who are "worse" than him. Neither does he pretend that what he did wasn't bad.

No, David owns his sin.

There are so many things that we could draw out of these particular verses, but I want to focus on just two main points. First of all, David knew that he was a sinner. He saw the ugly reality of his transgressions clearly laid out before him. Similarly, he looked over his shoulder and saw a trail of sin that wound all the way back to his very conception. And without hesitation he confessed it. He knew that if he was going to be rid of the wreckage in his life, he had to accept that it was his mess, and not someone else's, that needed clearing up.

Secondly, he saw that his sin was primarily an offence against God. Don't miss the magnitude of the statement: "Against you, you only, have I sinned". David's lack of self-control had led to a catalogue of evil events, including dereliction of duty, adultery, debauchery and eventually murder. His soldiers, Bathsheba, and her husband, Uriah, were all victims of his selfish decisions. And yet David claims that his sin is against God only.

That can't be right... can it?!

Look at this way—this is all a matter of worship. David's heart has strayed away from God and he had chosen instead to bow down to the idols of sex, power and reputation. As we discovered in Chapter Two, a king who builds idols instead of walls is doomed to fall, and fall he did. David, however, understood that while there were numerous people affected by his actions, ultimately it was God's law (and God's heart) that he had broken—and therefore it was God whom he had sinned against.

Committing sin is essentially cosmic adultery. It is an act of divine treason. The implications of this cannot be overstated. It means that in the sight of a God who is both just and perfect in every way, all of our sinful actions render us guilty, and there is nothing and no one that can change that.

However, it also means that if God, in his mercy, chooses to forgive us, then there is nothing and no one who can change that either.

Let me tell you why that's phenomenal.

I believe that what stops many guys from getting rid of their sin-wreckage is the belief that, because of those sins, they are unforgiven or unforgivable. That leads to lives marked by despair, brokenness, bitterness and shame. Consider the following:

- The unfaithful husband who has pleaded with his wife to forgive him but, such is her heartache, she refuses.
- The angry dad who keeps losing his temper with his kids. He has said sorry countless times, but the relationships seem broken beyond repair.
- The porn addict who has managed to keep his illicit online activities secret for years, yet whose soul remains crushed by guilt and shame.

What hope is there for these men? Will they experience peace and release if those they have sinned against offer forgiveness? A measure, perhaps. But what if they refuse? What then?

If forgiveness rests exclusively in the hands of the people we have sinned against, then we are all in big trouble, because few if any are either willing or able to give us the grace we crave. But if the sins of the unfaithful husband, the angry dad and the porn addict are primarily against God, then he has the power to declare them forgiven, clean and accepted, even if others don't.

That is a liberating and life-changing thought!

Brother, if there is murky sin in your life that you thought could never be moved, perhaps you have been looking in the wrong places for forgiveness. All of your sin is against God, so you need to bring it all to him because, as David discovered, he is an expert at clearing up our mess.

This gives you the freedom to own you sin and your responsibility. This gives you the freedom to bring it to God. This gives you the opportunity to know forgiveness.

Step three: GRACE—receive it

David is man enough to own his guilt, but once he's got it all off his chest and out in the open, he neither dwells on it nor wallows in self-pity. Instead, he receives and enjoys grace:

> Behold, you delight in truth in the inward being,
> and you teach me wisdom in the secret heart.
> Purge me with hyssop, and I shall be clean;
> wash me, and I shall be whiter than snow.
> Let me hear joy and gladness;
> let the bones that you have broken rejoice.
> Hide your face from my sins,
> and blot out all my iniquities.
> Create in me a clean heart, O God,
> and renew a right spirit within me.
> Cast me not away from your presence,
> and take not your Holy Spirit from me.
> Restore to me the joy of your salvation,
> and uphold me with a willing spirit. (v 6-12)

Again, David's language here is dripping with hope. Check out the words David uses: "purge", "clean", "wash", "blot out". These are the cravings of a dirty, sin-stained soul. David knew that his heart was rank dirty and crying out to be cleaned. The question is: how do you clean the human heart?

The only cleaning agent that David mentions is hyssop. Now chances are that you are not too familiar with hyssop, but its significance would not have been lost on David's Jewish audience. That's because the first reference to hyssop in the Bible is central to one of the most significant moments in Jewish history—the Passover. God had told every family in Egypt that their firstborn son would die that night. But he had something else to say to his people, through their leader Moses:

> Then Moses called all the elders of Israel and said to them,
> "Go and select lambs for yourselves according to your clans,
> and kill the Passover lamb. Take a bunch of hyssop and dip it
> in the blood that is in the basin, and touch the lintel and the
> two doorposts with the blood that is in the basin. None of you
> shall go out of the door of his house until the morning. For
> the LORD will pass through to strike the Egyptians, and when
> he sees the blood on the lintel and on the two doorposts, the
> LORD will pass over the door and will not allow the destroyer
> to enter your houses to strike you."   (Exodus 12 v 21-23)

The lambs died in the place of the firstborn sons, so that the
firstborn could live. The hyssop was what the household used
to paint the blood on their door, to show that they were trusting
that the lamb had died for their son.

And hyssop continued to be used by God's people once they had
escaped from Egypt. God knew they were unclean; so he allowed
them to sacrifice lambs to die in their place, just as he did back
in Egypt. Hyssop was used as part of the sacrificial ritual; it was
synonymous with sacrifice, mercy, deliverance and purification.

David recognised that his soul could only be clean—his life
could only be saved—by the blood of a lamb, applied to his soul.
He needing cleansing with hyssop. He needed the blood of a
lamb painted not round his door so much as over his heart.

Hold that thought, fast-forward a thousand years, and hear
the words of the prophet John the Baptist as he first lays eyes on
the man Jesus:

> Behold, the Lamb of God, who takes away the sin of the world!
> (John 1 v 29)

Here is the ultimate Lamb. Here is the One who can clear the
wreckage of the sin of anyone in the world—of David, of you and
of me. *But only if he dies.*

There are multiple references to hyssop in the Old Testament. There are only two in the entire New Testament. One, in Hebrews 9 v 19, refers to those sacrifices that were made in David's day. Here's the other:

> They took Jesus, and he went out, bearing his own cross, to the place called the place of a skull, which in Aramaic is called Golgotha. There they crucified him ...
>
> Jesus, knowing that all was now finished, said (to fulfil the Scripture), "I thirst." A jar full of sour wine stood there, so they put a sponge full of the sour wine on a hyssop branch and held it to his mouth. When Jesus had received the sour wine, he said, "It is finished", and he bowed his head and gave up his spirit. (John 19 v 16-18, 28-30)

Here is the Lamb, the sacrifice to end all sacrifices, brushed with hyssop. Here is the One who can take your place, bear your judgment, clean your heart, clear your wreckage.

Your only hope is David's hope—that God will forgive you because the Lamb died in your place. You and I must come to the cross. We must look at Jesus and say to his Father:

> Purge me with hyssop, and I shall be clean;
> wash me, and I shall be whiter than snow.

And we must know that God says: *Because of my Son's death, I will.*

It's a gift of staggering grace. You don't deserve it; you can't earn it. All you bring is your sin, your wreckage. What you receive is complete cleansing, a total clearing of all the mess, public and private, that your sin has caused.

That's grace. Have you received it?

Step four: GOALS—set them

Have you pictured what your life will look like when all the wreckage is cleared away and you have regained full control of it?

Think about that for a moment.

In the last chapter we saw that the ultimate goal is to be like Jesus. But for you, right now, in your life, in your context, what comes after forgiveness and restoration? In the closing lines of this psalm, David starts looking to the next steps and setting some goals. Check it out:

> Then I will teach transgressors your ways,
> and sinners will return to you.
> Deliver me from bloodguiltiness, O God,
> O God of my salvation,
> and my tongue will sing aloud of your righteousness.
> O Lord, open my lips,
> and my mouth will declare your praise.
> For you will not delight in sacrifice, or I would give it;
> you will not be pleased with a burnt offering.
> The sacrifices of God are a broken spirit;
> a broken and contrite heart, O God, you will not despise.
> Do good to Zion in your good pleasure;
> build up the walls of Jerusalem;
> then will you delight in right sacrifices,
> in burnt offerings and whole burnt offerings;
> then bulls will be offered on your altar.   (Psalm 51 v 13-19)

David can picture a life rebuilt, and it's compelling. In stark contrast to the deep shame and devastation that is evident in the opening verses of the psalm, grace has so liberated David that he now envisions himself teaching others so that they don't make the same mistakes that he did. He believes that loud, courageous praise will once again pour from his mouth. He sees a life marked by humility and sacrifice.

And he pictures a time when God will "build up the walls of Jerusalem". He is Israel's king; and a godly king, in God's strength, builds the walls. Forgiveness for his horrific lack of self-control will impact not only his own life, but the lives of those around him.

I love that this is the way that David closes out this psalm. Grace has changed the theme from the removal of wreckage to glorious restoration. That's what Jesus does!

So let's seek to be men who follow the example of King David. Don't fall into the trap of thinking that you can build anything of worth without first clearing the wreckage. And don't fall into the trap of thinking that you can clear the wreckage by your own efforts or good deeds, or by just hoping the passage of time will do it for you.

What is your wreckage? What will you do about it?

Turn to *God*.

Own your *guilt*.

Receive the *grace* of the cross.

Set gospel *goals*.

Don't think that you cannot build self-control because of your wreckage. However great the mess, Christ's cross is greater still. It's time to leave the wreckage with him, and to let him make us the self-controlled men we were born to be; the men we long to be, God wants us to be, and those close to us need us to be.

Brothers, it's time to build.

Tony's story

I was always quite a good, church-going boy. So, when I became a Christian at 19, I don't think I really grasped at all how amazing forgiveness was, or how much I needed it, or how incapable I was of living God's way by my own efforts.

Over the next two years, I found myself getting drunk time and time again. I'd repent each morning, but not really—I knew I'd get drunk again the next night, or the one after that. And as I lost control over that area of life, I began to slip in other areas, too.

It got to the stage where I stopped going to church, because I didn't want to hear what they said about my life. I veered between ignoring God, and then regretting what I'd done, but thinking that I was too far gone to be forgiven now.

Then one night, randomly, I was at a prayer night at which a really committed Christian prayed as Paul once had. He said he was the worst of sinners, but Jesus had come to save him. And it just hit me: no, I am the worst sinner in the room. I think before that moment, I'd never really thought of myself as a terrible sinner. I was like that for a few days, just feeling the weight of my sin. And then I remembered the other half of what that guy had said; and I realised that Jesus had come to forgive MY sin, ALL my sin.

It was one of the most liberating, as well as challenging, times of my life—to realise just what a sinner I am, and to begin to appreciate just what Jesus had done for me on the cross. Most of all, I remember the relief. There was a way back from my failure. There was a way out of my failure. And it all relied completely on what the Lord had done for me and would do for me, and not at all on anything I could or would do.

It's such a relief to admit you're a sinner, rather than trying to cover it up. And it's such a relief to know you're forgiven, whatever happens. I've realised that it's where life really starts.

5. Foundations

My hope is built on nothing less
Than Jesus' blood and righteousness;
I dare not trust the sweetest frame,
But wholly lean on Jesus' name.
On Christ, the solid Rock, I stand;
All other ground is sinking sand.

Edward Mote

Now we dig

So here we are, roughly at the midway point of a book that is all about building self-control into our lives, and so far we haven't even started laying bricks. We've assessed the ruins, considered the blueprint and excavated all the wreckage. Now we get the bricks in place, right?

No. Now we dig.

When it comes to construction I am by no means an expert, but my friend Jeff is. Jeff has been building houses since long before I was born, so there is very little that he doesn't knowing about building walls. And he would be the first to tell you that whatever it is you're looking to build, from hen houses to high-rise hotels, the key to buildings that last is the foundations.

I think that, however much building experience we have, most of us are aware that foundations are important, but the point really does need reinforcing. After all, when was the last time you entered a building of any description and marvelled at its foundations? Probably never!

More often than not, the physical appearance of what we can see—the brickwork, design features, fixtures and furnishings—are what get all the press. We can't see the foundations, so we rarely spare them a thought. However, for those who were fully engaged in the construction process, the foundations represent the most significant component of the whole project.

It's brutally simple. Get the foundations right, and the structure will be sound. Get the foundations wrong, and the building is compromised. The American songwriter David Allan Coe put it well when he said:

> "It is not the beauty of a building you should look at; it's the construction of the foundation that will stand the test of time."

There is deep wisdom in those words. Jeff assures me that solid foundations require two things: precise preparation and hard work. It's important that we keep that in mind as we launch into this foundational chapter. The purpose of this chapter is simply to identify the most suitable way for us to lay our foundations, so that we can get digging.

First of all, though, let me kick things off with this disclaimer—this is a not a complicated chapter. Rather, much like a house's foundation, what is presented here is very basic and unglamorous. But the principles that it lays out are most definitely deep and, if correctly applied, will ensure the strongest possible platform from which to start building towards your life of lasting self-control.

Christ is our foundation

We saw in Chapter Three that our blueprint is Jesus—being like him is our goal in all this. What I want to suggest now, however, is that Jesus is also our starting place. He is our foundation.

The notion of Jesus being a foundation upon which to build is a recurring theme throughout the Bible. In Psalm 118, the writer speaks of God's coming King, his Christ, in this way:

> The stone that the builders rejected has become the
> cornerstone. (v 22)

The cornerstone is the first stone to get laid in a building project. It is the point of greatest strength. Every other part of the structure begins with and rests upon the cornerstone. And in God's eternal building project—his people—he starts with a cornerstone:

> Look! I am placing a foundation stone in Jerusalem,
> a firm and tested stone.
> It is a precious cornerstone that is safe to build on.
> Whoever believes need never be shaken. (Isaiah 28 v 16 NLT)

Then Jesus comes along and, in the middle of a massive argument with the religious leaders who are rejecting him, he tells them that they will kill him, and asks:

> Have you not read this Scripture:
>
> > "The stone that the builders rejected has become the
> > cornerstone;
> > this was the Lord's doing, and it is marvellous in our
> > eyes"? (Mark 12 v 10-11)

See what he's saying? *You will reject me; you will kick me off the building site. But nevertheless I will be the foundation stone of God's people.*

Jesus is the only secure place where we can construct anything that lasts.

So how do we ensure that we are building on Christ as our foundation stone? Isaiah helps us out in that final line: "Whoever believes need never be shaken".

Believe!

It really is as simple as that.

1. Build on Jesus

Faith in Jesus is the key to a strong foundation.

It's crucial that we understand the importance of knowing Jesus at this stage in our venture. The heart of Christianity is not rules, traditions or instructions. It is a relationship with Jesus.

You've may have heard the line about Christianity being "a relationship, not a religion" before. You know it's about Jesus, not rules. And yet it is so easy to try to build self-control on the foundations of your own effort:

"I have just got to say no."

"OK, here are the new rules: no computer in my bedroom. No looking at girls as they walk past me. No more lads' mags or James Bond films. That'll stop my lust."

We look to our personal discipline and religious efforts. And if you do that, you may experience a measure of success. But it won't last. You're not building in the right place. You're not building deep enough, not laying solid foundations. Paul puts it like this:

> Why ... do you submit to regulations—"Do not handle, Do not taste, Do not touch!" ... These have indeed an appearance of wisdom ... but they are of no value in stopping the indulgence of the flesh.　　　(Colossians 2 v 20-23)

This kind of self-control is paper-thin and easily breached. It doesn't last—sooner or later you'll just break your own rules or forget how determined you were to resist temptation. Personal failure leads to despair: and if ever you succeed, success will give birth to pride at "mastering yourself", and we all know what pride comes before! Building on regulations produces walls "of no value".

God has something better for us than either of these outcomes. By building on Christ, we base our hope on a Saviour whose grace is such that he will never allow our moments of failure to condemn us to ruin, and whose power is so great that we will never have grounds for pride, as he alone will deserve the credit for any success in our lives.

We must fix our hope firmly on a Saviour, not a self-help programme.

Are you believing in Christ, or yourself? Is your anthem truly: "On Christ the solid rock I stand; all other ground is sinking sand"?

Christ is the foundation. But what does it actually mean to build on him?

2. Build on Jesus' words

My kids love building sandcastles. I love watching them on the beach with their little buckets and spades—digging, tipping, sculpting and decorating with sticks, shells and various crab appendages. Some of their sand-structures are truly magnificent!

Tragically, however, despite all of their efforts, not one of these spectacular beach-side palaces still stands today. Why? Because all sandcastles face the same, sad fate—the ocean will eventually creep up the beach like a silent, liquid ninja and test the true strength of the sandcastle's foundations.

There is only ever one winner!

The destruction of my kids sandcastles is a simple yet powerful reminder of the words of Jesus in Luke 6:

> Everyone who comes to me and hears my words and does them, I will show you what he is like: he is like a man building a house, who dug deep and laid the foundation on the rock. And when a flood arose, the stream broke against that house and could not shake it, because it had been well built. But the one who hears and does not do them is like a man who built a house on the ground without a foundation. When the stream broke against it, immediately it fell, and the ruin of that house was great. (v 47-49)

Jesus is laying out for us in no uncertain terms the key to strong, successful Christian living. Build your life on his word and you'll be able to stand against everything that comes at you. To build on anything else is madness, because all other ground, like sand, is dodgy and will eventually collapse beneath you. Now it's important to acknowledge here that Jesus is talking about the Christian life in general. However, if this principle applies to all areas of faith in Christ, it certainly applies to the area of self-control.

The word of God is foundational in building self-control that lasts.

And I don't think this just means that we need to search out verses that tell us to be self-controlled, or that tell us to resist one temptation or another, and remember them. I mean, do you really need to be told that you shouldn't get angry, get drunk, and so on? It's not that forgetfulness is our problem! Do you really need to be reminded that lusting after a woman is the same, in God's eyes, as sleeping with her? We know this!

Truth is, building on Christ's words means not only knowing his commands, but also enjoying his invitations—remembering not so much what we should do, but who we are. The Scripture tells us about what Jesus has done for us far more than it tells us what we ought to do for him. We need to remember that, otherwise the Bible is changed from being the Rock on which we build to the boulder beneath which we are crushed.

The writer Ed Welch put it brilliantly in an article in *The Journal of Biblical Counseling* back in 2001:

> "Scripture never expects us to hear God's commands to us in isolation from the serious contemplation of God's work for us in Christ."

Realising this has liberated me. The word of God has become fundamental to reconstruction in my life. Rather than simply dwelling on passages that say: "Dai, you need to do this" or: "Dai, you need to avoid that", I aim to focus on what Scripture tells me about who I am in Christ:

- God chose me to be holy and blameless before the foundation of the world (Ephesians 1 v 4).
- I am saved by God's grace, not my own good works (Ephesians 2 v 8-9).
- God will complete the work he has started in me (Philippians 1 v 6).
- My God will never leave or forsake me (Hebrews 13 v 5).
- Nothing can separate me from God's love (Romans 8 v 38-39).
- I am fully, irreversibly, 100% forgiven for ever (Isaiah 43 v 25).
- My God delights in me (Zephaniah 3 v 17).
- My sin doesn't disqualify me from salvation; it qualifies me to receive it (Mark 2 v 17).

- I am no longer a slave to sin; I have a new identity as a child of God (Galatians 4 v 7).

- God will use every situation, even my failures, for my good (Romans 8 v 28).

- I am a new creation (2 Corinthians 5 v 17).

- By Christ's death in my place, I am now the righteousness of God (2 Corinthians 5 v 21).

- The same Spirit that raised Jesus from the dead is at work in me (Romans 8 v 11).

- I have a glorious, sin-free, pain-free eternal future with Jesus to look forward to (Revelation 21 v 1-4).

Every one of these biblical nuggets has proved to be a solid foundation upon which my Christian life has been, and continues to be, built.

What are your verses? What precious promises straight out of the Bible do you turn to in moments of temptation or trial?

What are the biblical foundations that you are building on?

If you haven't got a lot of Scripture to build on—start finding precious verses now! No podcast, no counsellor, no worship track and no book (not even this one) are an adequate substitute for the rock of God's word. In all seriousness, put this book down RIGHT NOW, pick up a Bible, and spend some time reading God's word.

We build on Christ by making his word central to our view of who we are and why we're here.

But that's not enough...

3. Build on Jesus' work
The foundations upon which we build will be imbalanced and incomplete if we seek only to build on the person and words

of Jesus, because he is so much more than merely a good person and a wise teacher. Jesus is our Saviour, through what he has done for us in the gospel. Ultimately, our hope rests on the finished work of the Lamb's substitutionary death, burial and resurrection.

The apostle Paul drove this point home in a letter to a young, trainee pastor, Titus. Titus was seeking to lead a church in Crete; no easy task. We will learn more about Crete in the next chapter, but let's just say that, much like our current western culture, the people of Crete were insatiably indulgent and hedonistic, pursuing and approving of pretty much anything and everything that felt good. It was into this "anything goes" world that Paul wrote:

> For the grace of God has appeared, bringing salvation for all people, training us to renounce ungodliness and worldly passions, and to live self-controlled, upright, and godly lives in the present age, waiting for our blessed hope, the appearing of the glory of our great God and Saviour Jesus Christ, who gave himself for us to redeem us from all lawlessness and to purify for himself a people for his own possession who are zealous for good works. (Titus 2 v 11 - 14)

There is so much good stuff here. First, Paul reminds us of what we've already been looking at—that we should build upon the person of Jesus, the Saviour of the world who is, quite literally, the grace of God with skin on. Secondly, he re-affirms the centrality and strength of Jesus' words to equip and empower us to live self-controlled lives in the midst of a culture that has cast off all restraints. He then goes on to encourage us to look both to the glorious return of Christ and to his gracious redemption.

But notice what the grace of God trains us to do: "to live self-controlled, upright, and godly lives". Relying on and appreciating the work of Christ will enable us to build self-control that lasts. How?

a. Jesus died to redeem us from all lawlessness

This is huge! Jesus' cross was not just about providing forgiveness for our failures (which is awesome), but also about freeing us from our ferocious addiction to ungodly lusts and self-gratification. By his sacrificial death on the cross, Jesus has both paid the penalty and cancelled the power of our sin, liberating us to live a new kind of life—one that is marked by selflessness and self-control. Granted, there is still a war that rages each day that seeks to drag us back into a life of lawlessness, but no Christian can truly say: "I couldn't help it" or: "I was powerless to stop". In Christ we are redeemed (literally "bought out of slavery") from the old way of doing life. The battle is now to live in the power and reality of what Christ has already done for us on the cross.

The Christian man can look at temptation and say: *I have been redeemed. I don't have to give in. I'm free to resist.*

That's a truth you can build on!

b. Jesus died to purify us

We considered this in the previous chapter; but it's so significant that it's worth saying again and again. Jesus is committed to having a holy people who are his, and whose lives reflect that they are his. None of us could qualify were it left to us; but by the blood that he shed for us on the cross, we are cleansed from *all* sin, no matter how heinous, horrific or habitual it has been. The glory of the cross is that it doesn't sugar-coat our wretchedness. It shows just how grotesque our sin is and how it grieves the heart of God, while simultaneously showcasing the outrageous love of God for sinners like us. From the cross Jesus cried out: "It is finished!" It was the cry of a victorious champion. His salvation work truly is finished and the promise stands that:

> If we confess our sins, he is faithful and just to forgive us our sins and to cleanse us from all unrighteousness.

(1 John 1 v 9)

The eighteenth-century hymn-writer Charles Wesley put it this way: "His blood can make the foulest clean, his blood availed for me".

Guys who grasp this truth are unstoppable because, while failure might floor them momentarily, they know that in his grace Jesus will forever pick them up and clean them up again... and again... and again!

The Christian man can look at failure and say: *I have been purified. I can start again, again.*

That's a truth you can build on!

c. Jesus died to reconfigure our passions

I appreciate that you may be reading all this stuff about Jesus and what he's done for us, and it may be resonating with you, at least in part. However, I am also aware that a sense of scepticism and even fear may be creeping in right now as you start to think about what building on these truths might actually look like for you in practice.

Perhaps you're thinking:

> *"Dai, I believe all that stuff, I really do. But I also know full well what will happen next time my kids play up / that colleague flirts with me / I'm around alcohol / [insert your weakness here]. I know what's going to happen, Dai. I'm simply going to cave in to the same old passions that are burning out of control."*

If that's where you're at, Paul's closing words in this passage should really encourage you. Jesus died to redeem you... to purify you... so that you would be a man "zealous for good works". Zeal is a consuming passion. We're all zealous for something, passionate about something. The problem is not our zeal, but its object. It's like the American poet Jack Kerouac said:

"My fault, my failure, is not in the passions I have, but in my lack of control of them."

And so Paul is talking about how the gospel has the power to change our very nature. Jesus' work radically overhauls our "sinful DNA" and fully reconfigures our thoughts, appetites, drives and desires. Our passions are redirected towards Christ and living for him.

At the cross, we are confronted with a fierce brand of love that is above and beyond any other "pleasure" we could ever experience. The crucified Christ exposes every other idol as infinitely inferior, undeserving of our worship and incapable of satisfying our deepest cravings. By simply trusting in the finished work of the Lamb who loves us, we are transformed by liberating grace from being slaves to lust and idolatry into men who are free to worship our great God without shackles or shame.

The Christian says "no" to sin because in Christ we have a greater "yes"; because knowing Christ feels better and *is* better than disobeying him.

This is so different to a self-control built on self-effort, on a determination simply to say "no". Grace teaches me to look at sin and say: *I don't need this. I have something greater already. I have Christ. I don't need to enslave myself to this, because I am serving the Creator. Why would I waste my time on this when I can work for God? I'm not going to dress myself in these rags when I am already clothed in the righteousness, the perfection, of Christ.*

That's a truth you can build on!

And so here's the foundation of self-control: Jesus. We build on his word, and his work, and we live believing in him. Christ does not simply teach us; he changes us. His word teaches me that his work enables me to say to myself:

I am free to fight this temptation. I can be self-controlled.

I am forgiven when I give into temptation. I can still be self-controlled.

I am loved so much by the Creator that I don't want to give into this temptation. I love to be self-controlled.

That's how you start to build self-control that is joyful, real and lasting.

Ryan's story

My life before I knew Jesus was a mess. I used to sleep with prostitutes, almost every weekend, without fail. During this time, I was also addicted to drugs and watching pornography. My mind and my heart was a cesspit.

Then Jesus turned my world upside down. I heard that he took the punishment for all my filth so that I could be forgiven. But he didn't just forgive me—he had come to set the captives free. I needed that as much as forgiveness.

Some habits went instantly, like sleeping with prostitutes. Others took longer, like watching porn. I remember deeply repenting after watching some porn one night. I knew I was forgiven, but just wanted to live a life worthy of Jesus' calling.

I soon stopped watching porn completely, but there was one habit that took longer—masturbation. No matter how much I tried, I couldn't seem to stop this habit. I called out to God to help me again and again, but seemed to be stuck.

Then one day, I was in a church building and I saw a poster of a guy with shackles broken off his feet and a verse from the Bible above it saying: "For freedom Christ has set us free; stand firm therefore, and do not submit again to a yoke of slavery" (Galatians 5 v 1).

*It was in the past tense—he **has** set us free. I was free. Jesus had freed me from masturbation. So why was I still doing it?*

I noticed the second part—stand firm and don't submit again to a yoke of slavery. I had to exercise self-control. I was to stand firm in the knowledge and assurance that Christ had already set me free.

Over a period of about six months, as I stood against temptation, asking Jesus to give me the faith to believe that I was free, the control of the habit slowly loosened until finally I was living in freedom.

6. Gang

"Can we fix it?"

Bob the Builder

McQueen

With two adults, two boys and two girls in the Hankey house, picking a film for us all to watch together is not easy. In fact, there only seems to be one that is suitably manly for the boys, and suitably love-y for the girls:

Disney's *Cars*.

For the uninitiated, the plot (mild spoiler alert) revolves around an arrogant young hot-shot racing car, Lightning McQueen, who is set to become the first ever racing car to win the prestigious Piston Cup in his rookie season.

He has only one weakness—and it's his downfall, as he ignores his pit crew's call to come in for a tyre change. A double blowout on the final lap costs him victory and the Piston Cup, at least until the hastily-arranged tiebreaker race (but that's another story).

McQueen's problem is that he thinks he can do it on his own. After the race he is approached by veteran racing legend, the King, who has this advice for the young rookie:

"Hey, buddy. You're one gutsy racer. You got more talent in one lug nut than a lot of cars has got in their whole body...

But you're stupid. This ain't a one-man deal, kid. You need to
wise up and get you self a good crew chief and a good team.
And you ain't gonna win unless you got good folks behind
you, and you let them do their job, like they should."

The rest of the film is pretty much McQueen learning the truth of
the King's words. And (massive spoiler alert) *Cars* doesn't finish as
you'd expect, with a triumphant McQueen on the podium as the
Piston Cup winner. Instead, it finishes with a humble, gracious
McQueen surrounded by a team of faithful friends.

I share this story because in it I see the danger, but also the
hope, for us as men.

Whether we like to admit it or not, we are often like the
maverick McQueen. We are hard-wired to think that we can
manage on our own, and if we're honest, we are generally rubbish
at either asking for, or receiving help from others (just check our
track record in asking for directions, reading instructions and
going willingly to the doctor, if you need evidence!)

And maverick manhood is a dangerous place to be, especially
for Christian men.

One of my greatest fears in writing this book was that I might
(wrongly) convey a message that, with the right motivation and
the right course of action, you might somehow be able to build
walls of self-control alone. It would be an easy trap to fall into.
After all, this is a book that is all about self-control; the very
nature of the issue sounds like something that you need to deal
with yourself. Furthermore, you know as well as I do that the
true scale and shameful reality of just how out of control we
really are is largely known only to ourselves (as any consumer
of pornography will tell you). We may sin in private, and suffer
in private, and even confess in private. But we cannot deal with
these things in private.

So the message I am wanting to drive home here is both simple and radical:

Self-control is a team effort.

In fact, I want to make a bold, provocative and controversial claim:

Not only are "You" not enough to build self-control, but "You + God" is not enough either.

The true biblical formula is actually:

You + God + Others = Real and lasting change

We're in this together and we need each other. The strongest walls are built by gangs of "brickies" and, as we will see, it is only as we build together, in community, that we will be able to realise our dream of becoming the godly, self-controlled men that we long to be.

And that means church.

Church family

There are numerous places we could turn to in the Bible to explore the value and virtues of connecting with, committing to and serving in a local church. However, when it comes to considering what it might look like to build a life of self-control in the context of church community, it would serve us well to go back to Crete and listen to what Paul had to say to Timothy.

As we discovered in the last chapter, the prevailing culture in Crete was ferociously self-indulgent. Personal pleasure and self-gratification were pursued with reckless abandon by all sections of a morally bankrupt society that knew no limits and had cast off all restraints. This might sound harsh if it weren't a view shared by Cretan opinion-formers themselves, as Paul points out to Titus:

> One of the Cretans, a prophet of their own, said, "Cretans are always liars, evil beasts, lazy gluttons." (Titus 1 v 12)

Paul's vision for the church in Crete was for them to be different; to live radically counter-cultural lives marked by godliness and self-control.

However, Paul didn't only have a vision; he also had a strategy:

> But as for you, teach what accords with sound doctrine. Older men are to be sober-minded, dignified, self-controlled, sound in faith, in love, and in steadfastness. Older women likewise are to be reverent in behaviour, not slanderers or slaves to much wine. They are to teach what is good, and so train the young women to love their husbands and children, to be self-controlled, pure, working at home, kind, and submissive to their own husbands, that the word of God may not be reviled. Likewise, urge the younger men to be self-controlled. (Titus 2 v 1-6)

Paul knew that self-control would have to be a team effort. They were in it together and they needed each other. In these few verses Paul addresses older men, younger men, older women and younger women (I think that pretty much covers the whole church), identifying specific areas of vulnerability and potential weakness. It is clear from the things that Paul said to each group, both explicitly and implicitly, that at the heart of his concern for this church was the issue of self-control.

Here are a few observations and challenges we can draw from Paul's words, starting with the older men:

1. Be a father
Paul saw Titus as "my true child in a common faith" (1 v 4). You really get a sense that in writing these words of instruction

for the older men, Paul is essentially modelling to Titus what it means to be a true father in the faith, while demonstrating the value of exhorting others to do likewise. Paul wants his spiritual son, Titus, to raise up a generation of godly father-figures within the church who will take the younger men of the church under their wings and train them to be spiritually robust and self-controlled.

So if you're an older man, your self-control doesn't matter only for your sake, but for the younger men in your church. They need to be able to look up to you. They need to be able to learn from you. They need you to make yourself available to them, to be honest with them, to counsel them.

They need you.

2. Don't relax
Older men, Paul tells us, are to be sober-minded. Paul recognised the very real temptation to clock off and nod off, especially for men who work hard. But when it comes to self-control, there is no place for "pipe and slippers" in the Christian life, because it is when we are at our most complacent and lethargic that we are at our most vulnerable and susceptible to temptation. You don't retire from the fight for self-control until the day you die.

3. Set the tone
There is a reason why Paul addresses the older men first— because theirs is the mandate to lead, both in the home and in the church. It's the older men who set the tone. Against the backdrop of Cretan culture, a church served by dignified, self-controlled men as described by Paul would have been a secure and stable environment in which grace would prevail and faith would flourish. It's hard to envisage the women and especially the younger men excelling in self-control if the pillars of

church and home had not themselves exemplified self-control and noble character.

After addressing the older men, Paul then lays out some instructions for the ladies (a helpful reminder that being self-controlled is not only a challenge for men). He then speaks directly to the young guys...

1. Be self-controlled

Paul's word to Titus about the young men in his ranks was short, sharp and to the point: "Urge the younger men to be self-controlled". Simple as that. There is no point two or three, just: "Be self-controlled". The bottom line is this—a young man's greatest need is self-control, and his greatest failures often occur as a direct result of not having any. Impatience. Lust. Anger. Recklessness. Drunkenness. Ambition. Time-wasting. Self-control protects us from all of these.

As a young man I was stubborn, fiercely proud and strongly opposed to any kind of authority or advice (can you relate?) Many young men are both hard to lead and reluctant to follow, which is why they need pastoral input that is gracious, bold and consistent. Titus was to urge them to build walls of self-control within which they could grow, mature and honour Christ.

So if you're a younger man, are you willing to be urged to be self-controlled? Western culture exalts youth and sees advancing years as a weakness. The Scriptures do the opposite. Do you? Who are the older men who you ask to speak into your life, even when and where it hurts?

The gauntlet

Self-control is a church-wide project; we all have a part to play. So there is a need for each of us to answer this question honestly:

"Where am I at with church?"

I'm not just asking whether you're sat there Sunday by Sunday or not. I'm asking whether you're committed to the openness, the honesty, the risk and the reward of being in real community with the other members of your church.

Paul has in mind a church culture on Crete in which men can lead with courageous humility, and fail without fear of humiliation. Where older seasoned soldiers model godliness and train up young warriors to master youthful passions. Where sin can be confessed and grace administered. Where encouragement is contagious and comrades are committed to stirring one another on to love and good works. Where men can be men without being fake or fluffy. Where victories are won and celebrated as a unit, and the journey back from failure never has to be navigated alone. We must not be content with anything less than a church in which self-control is a team pursuit, and men are committed to building walls together.

God has in mind that church culture for your community, too. He gave you church because you need it, and it needs you.

So where are you at with church?

I appreciate that it is easy to look at church with a critical eye and a heavy heart. After all, our churches are groups of sinners who have been thrown into being family by their Saviour. It's not going to be perfect or easy!

But it's easy to complain. It's easy to see how others are not the committed, servant-hearted people your church needs. It's harder to be positive and proactive.

Truth is, if you want to see change, then you need to be that change. You can't transform how others see your church community or how they treat you. But you can ask God to transform you. You can be the older man or the younger man Paul called the Christian men of Crete to be.

Are you willing to pursue that vision and to make it reality? Will you play your part and allow others to do the same?

Will you let the church build the walls with you...

... and by doing so build up the church?

Christian friendship

As we have seen, meaningful connection to a local church is vital, not least meaningful connection with the men of the church. We need friends!

Scripture has so much to say about the power of Christian friendship. And it's so far from "Facebook friendship". True friendship , as the Bible defines it, is far more raw and robust than that. A true friend doesn't "unfriend" you, a true friend doesn't always have to "like" what you do, and a true friend doesn't only spend time with you at a time that suits them. Christian men share a common faith in a mutual friend, Jesus, and as such, our friendships should reflect something of his faithfulness, his courage and his grace. So let's recalibrate our view of friendship to line up with the Bible more than it reflects social media.

1. A true friend will go to war with you

I have several friends with military backgrounds and they all tell me the same thing—friendships forged in the trenches are unlike any other relationships they have known. Friends become family—brothers who would literally lay down their lives for each other. It's in the heat of battle that true friendship is forged.

What I love about this truth is that it perfectly captures the gospel heartbeat of the greatest friend of all, the One who went to war for us, King Jesus:

> This is my commandment, that you love one another as
> I have loved you. Greater love has no one than this, that
> someone lays down his life for his friends.　(John 15 v 12-13)

Jesus commands us to "love one another as I have loved you". The Christian life is lived out in a war zone, and every day we come under fire—the relentless bombardment of temptation, the paralysing fear of screwing up again, the agony and shame of defeat. Our battle for self-control is bloody, brutal and more than we can handle on our own. But we don't stand alone. True friends are alongside us in the fight.

Who are the friends who fight with you and for you? Who are the fellow Christians you would lay your life down for, and who do you lay down your time, your energy and your comfort for? Who are your brothers in arms?

2. A true friend speaks truth, even when it hurts

A few years ago my friend, Steve, challenged me to try to lose 8% of my body weight. Essentially, he was telling me I was fat! I was not hugely obese, but I had started to pile on the pounds. And it was an issue of self-control. I loved extra helpings more than I loved looking after the body God has given me, and more than I cared about being around long-term to lead my family.

Despite my initial shock, I remember feeling very grateful that Steve had been bold enough to speak into this area of my life. I imagine others had noticed my weight gain—only Steve took the risk of talking to me about it.

Self-control cannot be achieved alone. Somehow, each day I had been able to look at the man in the mirror and not notice that he was getting bigger. It took the courageous intervention of a compassionate brother to help me face reality and set the agenda for change.

Your issue may not be your weight; perhaps it's your temper, your work life or your fixation with technology. Whatever it is, you need discerning friends who have both the love and the licence to call you on it before you're out of control. As the Scriptures put it: "Faithful are the wounds of a friend" (Proverbs 27 v 6).

Who are the friends you have whom you allow to be close enough to you to do this? Have you given them permission so they know that you know that you need this?

3. A true friend makes you stronger

Two are better than one, because they have a good reward for their toil. For if they fall, one will lift up his fellow. But woe to him who is alone when he falls and has not another to lift him up! Again, if two lie together, they keep warm, but how can one keep warm alone? And though a man might prevail against one who is alone, two will withstand him—a threefold cord is not quickly broken. (Ecclesiastes 4 v 9-12)

This passage paints a stunning picture of friendship for us. We work better and fight harder when we do so together. We are far better positioned to experience restoration, share comfort and celebrate victory if we are striving together. A three-fold cord—two Christians, united by their faith in Christ—is a strong rope.

These words totally resonate with me. Whether it's brothers I've known for years, loyal leaders, or members of my church family, not to mention my wife, I would not be the man that I am today were it not for my friends. I thank God for them all.

Get connected

As we draw this chapter to a close, I'm hoping that the task of rebuilding the walls now looks different to when you started. Sure, becoming a man of self-control is going to be a huge undertaking, but how reassuring it is to recognise that you don't have to do this alone. And how humbling it is to realise that you are unable to do this alone.

You are surrounded by church family and friends, men and women, young and old, who are fighting the same battles, craving the same transformation, clinging to the same grace and on the same team as you.

Don't be a maverick. You need them. They need you.

Build together.

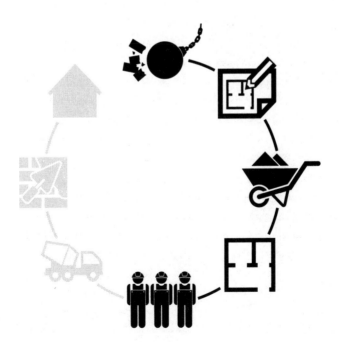

Marvin's story

I can't really overstate how valuable the support of my Christian brothers has been in helping me tackle an area of sin in my life, namely masturbation, fuelled by pornography.

Since my early teens I had steadily cultivated a habit of secret lust, in spite of already being a Christian. I was aware it was wrong, and on each occasion I was repentant. Yet because I never confessed the sin to anyone other than God, I was able to delude myself that I could get it defeated alone. And besides, I thought I was the only one disobeying in this area. So the habit grew, and the lingerie section of my mum's clothing catalogue was replaced by internet nudity and sex scenes.

It was only at university, when I was sharing a house with a couple of other Christian students, that things began to change. At some point masturbation was mentioned, it opened up a conversation, and for the first time I realised I wasn't the only one trying (and failing) to fight this.

Around that time I was invited to meet up weekly with two godly Christian guys for prayer and something called "accountability". It sounded a bit mad, but really it was what I longed for—Christian friends who cared enough about me to check up on how I was really doing, and not let me keep papering over my sin. I found my struggles became easier to overcome because I wasn't doing it alone.

Ever since then, I've made it a priority to seek out Christian men who I can trust to help me wage war on my sin. Confessing sins to others goes a long way towards breaking the grip of unhealthy habits, and regular prayer and encouragement from others gives strength at times of failure. I don't find it comes naturally to bare my soul and struggles—it's risky, it's awkward, and it's always easier to stay silent. But opening up has in turn opened up a channel for God's grace in my life—the gift of my brothers in Christ and their powerful prayer support.

7. Cement

The gospel is a gift that comes with "batteries included".

Tim Chester

Crunch

It was very late. It was very dark. It was raining. I was exhausted.

They're my four best excuses for why I crashed my car into a wall that evening. Actually, I only really nudged it as I pulled out of the parking space. Yet when I got out to look, the wall looked as if it had been hit by a hand grenade. Bricks and debris were literally strewn everywhere.

As word got out that the local pastor had just smashed up a brand new wall in the car park, unsurprisingly people started coming to have a look. But their comments to me were less along the lines of:

"Why don't you learn how to drive properly?"

and more like:

"Wow! What kind of cement did those cowboys use?!"

The huge pile of sandy rubble told its own story. The wall might have looked impressive when first constructed, but as soon it was put to the test, it was found wanting. The weakness, it would seem, was not the bricks that had been used, but rather the sub-standard mortar. When it came to the literal crunch, it simply wasn't strong enough to hold the wall together.

This story illustrates two things. First, I'm a rubbish driver. Secondly (and more importantly for this chapter) strong walls require solid cement.

With the foundation of Christ in place, we are ready at last to build. In the final chapter we are going to get to grips with some of the practical bricks that we can use to build walls of lasting self-control. However, this chapter is in many ways the most important chapter of the book, because it's all about ensuring that we are using the correct cement. If we get this part of the project wrong, then despite all our hard work in confession, repentance and rebuilding, the walls that we construct are ultimately condemned to collapse. Get it right, however, and we will be building something formidable.

So here's the question: what is the cement that we so vitally need? Well, it's not so much a question of *what* is the cement as *who* is the cement.

And the answer is: the Holy Spirit. We need a team around us as we build self-control. But we need even more the Spirit working within us as we build.

God's gift to change us

Ezekiel's prophecy in the Old Testament was written in a time of frenzied spiritual rebellion. God's people had collectively turned their backs on him, choosing instead to pursue the idols and pagan practices of the surrounding nations. In staggeringly graphic detail, Ezekiel 23 likens the nation of Israel to a whore who, burning with lust and enslaved by vulgar passions, has repeatedly "cheated" on her faithful lover—God—breaking his heart again and again.

It was this adultery that had ended up with Jerusalem's walls being breached one final, catastrophic time. Ezekiel spoke to God's people in Babylon, in exile in a foreign city. In his grace, however, God chose to reach out to his out-of-control people, promising to bring them back to their land, back into relationship with him.

But there was still a problem. The people had proved that they could not live God's way. What good would it do them to come back to their towns, only to rebel and face judgment all over again? How would things be any different?

In chapter 36, God explains what he is going to do:

> I will sprinkle clean water on you, and you shall be clean
> from all your uncleannesses, and from all your idols I will
> cleanse you. And I will give you a new heart, and a new spirit
> I will put within you. And I will remove the heart of stone
> from your flesh and give you a heart of flesh. And I will put
> my Spirit within you, and cause you to walk in my statutes
> and be careful to obey my rules. (Ezekiel 36 v 25-27)

At the heart of Israel's wretchedness were their wretched hearts. If they were going to truly change, what they needed was nothing less than a heart transplant, a radical re-wiring of their desires and devotions. No one can give themselves a heart transplant; so God promised to do the surgery through his Spirit, who would empower his people to live in a godly way that would have otherwise been impossible.

Several millennia later, the hearts of men are no different to those of Ezekiel's contemporaries. Mercifully, the heart of God has not changed either. His offer of gospel heart-surgery and Holy Spirit renewal still stands. And we still need it.

The mere mention of the Holy Spirit can conjure up a wide range of thoughts and responses. The whole question of what we should expect the Spirit to do has become something, sadly, of a battleground and a subject that divides Christians. But here, we simply need to grab from Ezekiel the answers to two questions:

- How do I receive the Holy Spirit?
- What does the Holy Spirit do?

1. How do I receive the Holy Spirit?

There is much confusion as to how we actually receive the Holy Spirit. Does it happen during those intense moments of worship in church? Does it need a godly pastor-type person to lay their hands on us? Is it a one-shot deal, or do we have to get topped up on a regular basis?

"I will put my Spirit within you," says God. Jesus fills out how this happens:

> That which is born of the flesh is flesh, and that which is
> born of the Spirit is spirit. Do not marvel that I said to you,
> "You must be born again." (John 3 v 6-7)

It is the third person of the Trinity, the Holy Spirit, who causes us to be born again. Each one of us has been born naturally "of the flesh"—physically alive, but spiritually dead, like spiritual zombies! However, when we place our faith in Jesus, rejecting our dead way of life and trusting him to save us, something incredible happens—we get "born again to a living hope through the resurrection of Jesus Christ from the dead" (1 Peter 1 v 3). In other words, we get de-zombified!

It is the Holy Spirit who brings about this new birth and then takes up residency in our hearts.

So if you believe in Jesus, you have the Spirit. The only reason you believe in the Son is because you have the Spirit. Every true disciple has the Spirit, fully, guaranteed. Once you're born, you're born.

2. What does the Holy Spirit do?

The Spirit lives within us to motivate and empower us to live God's way. He is committed to making us look and live like our Saviour, Jesus, who, as we saw in Chapter Two, is the epitome of self-control. The Spirit frees us to be the people we were designed to be.

> Now the Lord is the Spirit, and where the Spirit of the Lord is, there is freedom. And we all, with unveiled face, beholding the glory of the Lord, are being transformed into the same image from one degree of glory to another. For this comes from the Lord who is the Spirit.   (2 Corinthians 3 v 17-18)

This is what is called sanctification. We are all works in progress and, thankfully, the Holy Spirit is in it for the long haul. The words in Ezekiel 36 v 27 tell us that it is the Holy Spirit who "causes" us to walk in a new, God-honouring way.

What's wrong with me then?

But if all this is true, then why do we mess up? If the Spirit lives in you and me, and is committed to changing us "from one degree of glory to another", then why is self-control still so hard to attain?

Tim Chester helpfully writes that:

> "The gospel is a gift that comes with 'batteries included'."

In other words, when God saves us, he doesn't just command us to live a new kind of life; he also gives us the power that we need to be able to do so by the Holy Spirit. We get the batteries included. However, having bought more irritating electronic gadgets, games and gizmos for my children than is good for the sanity of any family, I can testify that it's one thing to have a toy with a set of fully-charged batteries; it's quite something else to know how to fit them and get the thing to work!

The Christian life can be a bit like that. The batteries are included; but they need to be fitted.

I became a Christian as a teenager. I had no clue what power was now available to me. I knew that Jesus had jumped into the cesspit of my sin, lifted me out, cleaned me up and put me on the rescue helicopter marked "heaven". But, in my understanding, he'd then handed me the controls and said: *You take it from here, brother! I saved you, now it's over to you—don't mess up!*

It was not long until I crashed and burned.

In fact, for many years my Christian life looked something like this: failure, shame, repentance, restoration, fresh resolve... failure (repeat).

It was exhausting, exasperating... and unnecessary!

I genuinely had no idea that God was not only involved at the point of my salvation; he was also 100% committed to the process of my sanctification. I did not know that he was more dedicated to transforming my train-wreck of a life than I was. Don't get me wrong, I knew that I had been saved by grace, but I was now trying to live a godly life and keep God's rules in my own strength.

And it was futile. I had traded in the riches of God's grace for the rags of religion. I was saved but still enslaved. Converted but still out of control.

Does that sound at all familiar to you? If so, you're not alone. A bunch of Christians in first-century Galatia were going through exactly the same thing.

Paul was very blunt:

> Let me ask you only this: Did you receive the Spirit by works
> of the law or by hearing with faith? Are you so foolish?

> Having begun by the Spirit, are you now being perfected by
> the flesh?   (Galatians 3 v 2-3)

Paul wanted to help the Galatian believers recognise the insanity of living by what he called "works of the law", living by their own efforts; he longed for them to see that their attempts to live for God without using the power of God were foolishness.

We would do well to heed his advice today. No matter how sincere our motives and no matter how hard we struggle, we will *never* become men of self-control by our own efforts. We simply cannot achieve what only the Holy Spirit is capable of achieving.

The everyday war-zone

Acknowledging that self-control is impossible aside from the gracious graft of the Holy Spirit within us is the most liberating truth for us as men seeking to rebuild broken walls. However, it does not make the struggles that we face any less real or relentless. Simply acknowledging that I can't do it, and believing that God can, does not change the fact that I'm still tempted to watch stuff I shouldn't when I'm up late, I still find it hard to see my kids beyond my smartphone when I'm tired, and I still feel like knocking out the driver who cuts me up when I'm in a rush.

I know that I'm pathetically weak. I need to know that the Holy Spirit is powerful. And I need to know what has got to happen for me to see his transformational power unleashed in my life.

Paul's encouragement to the Galatians here is stunning:

> But I say, walk by the Spirit, and you will not gratify the
> desires of the flesh. For the desires of the flesh are against

the Spirit, and the desires of the Spirit are against the flesh, for these are opposed to each other, to keep you from doing the things you want to do. But if you are led by the Spirit, you are not under the law. Now the works of the flesh are evident: sexual immorality, impurity, sensuality, idolatry, sorcery, enmity, strife, jealousy, fits of anger, rivalries, dissensions, divisions, envy, drunkenness, orgies, and things like these. I warn you, as I warned you before, that those who do such things will not inherit the kingdom of God. But the fruit of the Spirit is love, joy, peace, patience, kindness, goodness, faithfulness, gentleness, self-control; against such things there is no law. And those who belong to Christ Jesus have crucified the flesh with its passions and desires. If we live by the Spirit, let us also keep walk by the Spirit.

(Galatians 5 v 16-25)

There is a war that rages within each Christian, between "the Spirit" and "the desires of the flesh"—the natural me that wants to do whatever looks good and feels good, rather than what God says is good. The Spirit and the flesh are "opposed to each other". So the Christian life is about conflict. If you don't fight, you've lost. If you know you're in a war-zone, be encouraged—that's Christian normality.

When we're honest, we can all identify some of the "works of the flesh" that Paul lists. And here's the thing: they're all hallmarks of being out of control. Shamefully, I'm all too familiar with all too many of them. So are you.

So I love this passage. The Spirit is with us, fighting for us, committed to growing in us the "fruit of the Spirit". It's a "multi-tasty" fruit. It tastes of love, joy, peace, patience, kindness goodness, faithfulness, gentleness and... wait for it... SELF-CONTROL!

Growing fruit

I was privileged to grow up in a home with a large garden and a green-fingered father who loved growing fruit. And I made two non-revolutionary observations:

- Apple trees never grew cherries and strawberry plants never sprouted raspberries. They produced fruit according to their kind.

- None of the plants, trees or bushes ever seemed to struggle to bear fruit—they just kept popping it out at the right time.

These simple observations help us better to understand how the Holy Spirit works, and how he can help us to start producing what the American pastor John Piper calls "the fierce fruit of self-control".

Apple trees grow apples. Strawberry plants grow strawberries. The Spirit grows the fruit of the Spirit. It's who he is, so it's what he produces. If we have received the Holy Spirit, we should expect a harvest of his fruit in the same way as my dad expected a harvest of apples and strawberries every year.

Trying to cultivate self-control without God's help is both draining and debilitating because it's impossible. But it's not hard work for the Holy Spirit, who is abounding in all that is good, godly and Christ-like, not least self-control.

So what must we do for the Holy Spirit to bear fruit in our lives?

Quite simply, we must let him!

Look at the language used by Paul throughout this passage. "Walk by the Spirit" (v 16, 25). Be "led by the Spirit" (v 18).

If we are going to become self-controlled men, we must simply get on board with what the Holy Spirit is already doing, instead of getting in his way. We must let him bear his fruit in us.

And he specialises in self-control.

Partners with the Spirit

Now the danger at this point would be to embrace the truth that self-control is the Holy Spirit's job and to conclude that this somehow lets us off the hook; that we simply let him do his thing while we kick back, chillax and puff away on a victory cigar. But that would be a cataclysmic mistake. Yes, life change is God's work, but our role is not passive apathy, but active partnership. Paul put it this way in his letter to the Philippians:

> Therefore, my beloved, as you have always obeyed, so now, not only as in my presence but much more in my absence, work out your own salvation with fear and trembling, for it is God who works in you, both to will and to work for his good pleasure. (Philippians 2 v 12-13)

Our work is to let him work his desire to work in us!

Let me use an image to try to explain this. I love it when my kids come home from school and tell us that they've been given a craft project. The reason I love it is because my wife, Michelle, is a junk-modelling genius. Give her a cereal box, a washing-up bottle, a couple of toilet rolls and a roll of sticky tape, and there is nothing that she can't make. It's incredible to watch her at the dining table directing the kids in their snipping, colouring and sticking, as she helps them to build whatever random object or creature they've been tasked to create. My kids have never taken a model into school that was anything less than phenomenal. As their dad, it really is fantastic to see them so chuffed with what they've made, to hear their teachers commend their work and listen to their mates congratulate them on what they've achieved. And yet I know the truth. I know that if it weren't for their amazing mum patiently and lovingly equipping, empowering and encouraging them behind the scenes, the outcome would look very different.

In the same way, this is what it looks like for us to work in partnership with the Holy Spirit. He is the one who has all the skill, all the power and all the encouragement that we need, but we still need to be faithful to snip, colour, stick and build as he directs us. No one can bring about real, lasting self-control in the life of a dysfunctional man... except the Spirit.

Brothers, as we step into the next chapter and finally get our hands on the building blocks that we need to get these walls of self-control built, let's do so in absolutely no doubt that whatever we seek to construct from this point forward, it needs to be permeated throughout, and thoroughly held together, by the power of the Holy Spirit.

Without him, anything and everything will knock our walls down. With him, we can withstand anything.

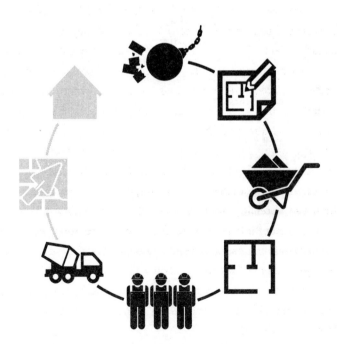

Simon's story

I had engaged in the battle to be a self-controlled, authentic and integral man many times; and I had failed many, many times to be the man I knew God wanted me to be. I was doing loads of "church stuff", had accountability partners, prayer groups, "Covenant Eyes" software on my laptop, I'd made promises to God and to myself; and ultimately it all failed because, at the end of the day, I was fighting in my strength.

One day I was sat in my room, overcome with defeat. I just cried out to God. In an instant, the darkness around me became light; it felt like chains had been removed. I knew Jesus had died for me and that I had been given the righteousness of Christ in a really tangible, experiential way. This was a mountain-top experience of the Holy Spirit sanctifying me.

This experience of the presence of God enabled me to be really self-controlled—or you might say, Spirit-controlled—for a long time after that. It was like someone gave me self-control steroids, and I look back on that time of my life with the greatest joy at the memories of the precious times I had with God, and the habits he was building into my life.

So what happened after that? I went on to live a sinless and holy life and live happily ever after? No—I had to realise that I am called to live life in the valley, not on the mountain-top, daily seeking the power of the Spirit, daily failing, and daily repenting. I'm not saying that it is impossible to have beautiful seasons of knowing the rapid, changing work of the Spirit, and when those times come, I am so grateful. But I also remember that in the battle and the daily slog God is still at work, and the Spirit is at work in me and for me still.

8. Bricks

I'm gonna reconstruct, brick by brick.

Arctic Monkeys

Brick by brick

Like many Welshmen, I visited a lot of castles during my childhood. I used to love racing up the towers and re-enacting battle scenes with sticks for swords (and now I'm a dad, I get to do it all over again!) Castles have always fascinated me because they have stood strong for so many centuries, and because of the incredible feat of engineering that each castle represents. To think that these mighty fortresses were built before the age of heavy plant machinery and power tools is staggering. Each individual brick and block had to be painstakingly measured, cut, shaped and laid by the hands of diligent craftsmen.

Brick by brick. That's how those workers built.

The construction of these castles took many years to complete. There was no other way. No shortcuts to success. Once built, however, there was nowhere safer, more secure or more spectacular to live. The fact that people still flock to visit these buildings today tells you all you need to know about the enduring quality of what those medieval workmen achieved.

Self-control is something that only the Holy Spirit can achieve in us; but we still have to join him on site and get involved. So this chapter will consider some of the different building blocks that God has given us to work with, all of which have been hewn from the solid rock of Scripture.

What follows will be far more practical than any of the previous chapters; maybe it's the one you've been waiting for, and you'd begun to wonder if it would ever come! However, I hope that you now realise why the section about what you have to do has been preceded by the infinitely more important sections on what God has already done in his Son, and continues to do for you through his Spirit.

(By the way, if you have skipped the first seven chapters of the book and come straight here, you are cheeky and you need to repent and go back to the beginning. Thanks.)

Just as with the construction of those mighty Welsh castles, there are no shortcuts to success in all this. We are going to have to build walls of self-control in exactly the same way those stone-masons of old built.

Brick by brick.

However, before we get to the bricks, let's get specific. Ask yourself:

In what three areas of my life am I most lacking in self-control right now?

1. _____

2. _____

3. _____

It would be good for you to have these three issues in mind as you start handling these bricks.

Brick #1: Alertness

Sunday evening after a long day of ministry with my church family is the most dangerous time of the week for me. I'm physically smashed, emotionally drained, spiritually spent and all I want to do is put my feet up... and let my guard down. It's at that very moment that, like a boxer with low hands, I'm an easy target. My mind starts to wander, my tongue gets loose and my discernment goes AWOL. I become prone to wasting time on social media, speaking unkindly to others, and making unwise decisions about what I look at and listen to.

Sunday evening is when I'm at my most vulnerable. So it's when I need to be at my most alert.

What about you? When are you at your most vulnerable in the three areas you've identified? Is it when you are worn out, or ticked off, or cast down, or stressed out, or sexually frustrated?

Whenever it is, be aware that your enemy, the devil, knows too; and he has systems and strategies in place to take you down. We are never more in danger than when we think we are safe, as Paul pointed out:

> Let anyone who thinks that he stands take heed lest he fall.
>
> (1 Corinthians 10 v 12)

That's why, in one sense, success is also so dangerous. You know how it goes—you win a mini-victory over a sinful habit, it seems the war is won, and then before you know it, your self-control has failed, the enemy has breached the wall, and there's a wreckage that needs clearing up.

So what can we do to stand firm? Peter has some solid advice for us on this:

> Be sober-minded; be watchful. Your adversary the devil
> prowls around like a roaring lion, seeking someone to
> devour. Resist him, firm in your faith.   (1 Peter 5 v 8-9)

We need to be alert. Do you look out for temptation, and name it for what it is—an attack from Satan? Do you know your moments of greatest weakness? What would being watchful look like for you in your areas of struggle?

Brick #2: Brutality

So we need to be vigilant; we also need to be violent.

Allow me to illustrate. A few years ago a rat moved into our attic. Let me tell you what we didn't do:

- We didn't ignore it.
- We didn't befriend it and make it a pet.
- We didn't try to empathise with its needs and desires.

No, we set traps. And when the rat's cheese-lust finally lured him into one of them, we celebrated!

This is how we should be dealing with our sin. Galatians 5 v 24 tells us that:

> Those who belong to Christ Jesus have crucified the flesh
> with its passions and desires.

Did you catch the violence of that phrase? Crucified. Executed. Killed.

I am convinced that one of the main reasons we don't experience more victory over sin is because we don't kill it. We let ourselves think about sinning in some way. We walk right up close to actually sinning, thinking we can stop before we disobey. We repent of a sin while leaving all the means in place to sin in that way again. We show it mercy when we should be murdering it!

God commands us:

> Make no provision for the flesh, to gratify its desires.
>
> (Romans 13 v 14)

Be brutal with a sin. Kill it. Don't leave it lying around, ready to be picked up sometime when you're weak.

Joseph needs to be our model here. There he is, in a privileged position in an Egyptian household, and his master's wife grabs him and says: "Lie with me" (Genesis 39 v 12). What does Joseph do? He is self-controlled. He doesn't have sex with her. But he doesn't hang around either, leaving himself the option of giving in later. "He left his garment in her hand and fled and got out of the house" (v 12). He got out. Joseph ended up going to prison, accused of attempted rape. He lost his freedom; but he did not lose his purity.

What does it look like to murder our sin? Here are a few examples from my own life:

- After years of slavishly consuming hours upon hours of mind-numbing, soul-destroying, smutty TV, I eventually realised that the only way to break the habit was to get rid of my TV altogether. I haven't had TV in my house now for over 15 years.

- Being a man who has always struggled to drink alcohol in moderation, a shameful night of drunken disgrace some 14 years ago resulted in deep repentance and a decision to never drink alcohol again. By God's grace I have been sober ever since.

Some people find my actions extreme. And I completely agree with them. But crucifixion is extreme, and that's what this is all about. The Puritan John Owen put it starkly and truthfully:

> "Be killing sin or it will be killing you."

I love what Ed Welch wrote on this in his book *Addictions*:

> "There is a mean streak to authentic self-control.
> Underneath what seems to be the placid demeanour of
> those who are not ruled by their desires is the heart of a
> warrior. Self-control is not for the timid. When we want to
> grow in it, not only do we nurture an exuberance for Jesus
> Christ, we also demand of ourselves a hatred for sin."

Are you polite to your sin? Or brutal with it? Your brutality won't look the same as mine—we're different, and our walls are weakest at different places. But look back to your three answers on page 90, and identify how you are going to build self-control by killing your sin. What might it look like for you?

- Do you need to stay offline after a certain time or start using accountability software?
- Are there unhelpful influences you need to steer clear of for a while (or for ever)?
- Is it time to stop chasing that promotion and spend more time with your family?
- Should you delete your Facebook account?
- Do you need to speak to your pastor about anger management counselling?
- Might now be a good time to go on a diet or start exercising more?

Brick #3: Word

Fundamental to self-control is a firm grip on God's word, as we saw Jesus stunningly demonstrate back in Chapter Three, as he was tempted in the wilderness. If the Son of God needed Scripture to withstand temptation, how much more do we?

> How can a young man keep his way pure?
> By guarding it according to your word.
> With my whole heart I seek you;
> let me not wander from your commandments!
> I have stored up your word in my heart,
> that I might not sin against you.   (Psalm 119 v 9-11)

These helpful and hopeful words are clear. We need to be men of the Book! We are protected from impurity by the Scriptures. We are kept on the straight and narrow by the truth. And the key to living a sin-slaughtering, Christ-exalting life is to stuff our hearts with the liberating word of God.

In the Bible we meet incredible heroes like Joseph and Daniel, whose faith and devotion should inspire us to stand strong. Every gospel truth believed, every promise clung to and every command obeyed effectively galvanises our faith and fortifies our lives. Scripture is absolutely essential to us as we seek to build lives of lasting self-control.

- What are the Scriptures that most apply to your three area of weakness? (If you're not sure, when will you speak to an older Christian or your pastor for some guidance?)

- Which gospel nuggets will you turn to when you're next tempted?

- What are you doing to increase your stockpile of biblical bricks?

- What might it look like for you to invite others to speak God's word into your life?

Brick #4: Prayer

God speaks to us through his word. Prayer is how we speak to God. The greatest pray-er who ever lived is Jesus, which prompted one of his disciples to ask him: "Lord, teach us to pray" (Luke 11 v 1). Jesus' response was to lay out a model prayer:

> Father, hallowed be your name.
> Your kingdom come.
> Give us each day our daily bread,
> and forgive us our sins,
> for we ourselves forgive everyone who is indebted to us.
> And lead us not into temptation.   (Luke 11 v 2-4)

Whatever your three areas of weakness, you will find that each line of this prayer has something profound to say about the challenge of building self-control that lasts.

a) God's glory is primary in my life

"Father, hallowed be your name." This opening line blows clean out of the water any sense of pride or personal swagger that we may have. It reminds us that our goal in becoming self-controlled men should be nothing less than our faithful Father receiving all the honour and adulation for the miraculous work that he has performed in our lives.

Pray that God would get all the glory for the transformation in your life.

b) God's purposes supersede my passions

"Your kingdom come." Jesus wants us to recognise that true gospel

change can only occur by way of divine invasion. Jesus is daring us to pray a prayer that is both courageous and dangerous—a prayer that gives him the green light to come and have his way in us. To put his agenda above our own and to make his purposes a higher priority than our passions.

Ask God to establish his kingdom in the three areas of challenge you have identified.

c) God's provision is all that I need

"Give us each day our daily bread." What is it that you need in order to become the man of God you aspire to be? By praying "give us each day our daily bread", we acknowledge three key truths:

- Only God can truly satisfy our desires and fulfil our cravings.
- Our dependence upon God's gracious provision is a daily reality.
- He is a generous Father, who loves it when we ask for help.

Humble yourself every day by inviting God into your struggle and asking him to satisfy your needs.

d) God's forgiveness covers my failures

"And forgive us our sins..." As much as we should both expect and experience God's sanctifying work in our lives, the hard truth is that we will still screw up! There is forgiveness for all our failures and mercy for every mistake.

Deal decisively with your sin by repenting quickly and receiving God's grace.

e) God's grace sets me free

"... for we ourselves forgive everyone who is indebted to us." Grace changes us, and that is incredible! However, grace also breathes freedom and forgiveness into our broken relationships. If grace can liberate us to such a degree that we are able to gladly love and willingly forgive those who have wronged us, there are surely no limits to what else the power of the gospel can achieve in our lives and relationships.

Pray for God's grace to set you free and for that freedom to impact others.

f) God's deliverance is available

"And lead us not into temptation." Have you ever known such fierce temptation that it seemed more a case of when, rather than if, you were going to lose control? Ever listened to the lie (and it is a lie): *You're going to give in eventually, so you may as well give in now?*

If so, learn to pray at those moments. And learn to cling onto the truth (and it is true) that God is always giving you a way out:

> God is faithful, and he will not let you be tempted beyond
> your ability, but with the temptation he will also provide the
> way of escape, that you may be able to endure it.
>
> (1 Corinthians 10 v 13)

Whether your need is increased strength, enhanced will-power, wisdom beyond your years or divine intervention, God has got your back when you are confronted with temptation.

When you are tempted, make prayer your first port of call rather than your last resort.

Brick #5: Discipline

The fifth brick that we need to get our hands on is discipline, because when it comes to self-control that lasts, this is so often where the wheels come off. Whether it's the gym membership we had to cancel or the diet that lasted right up until we walked past that fast-food restaurant, our good intentions mean very little if they are not backed up by a disciplined life. As we've seen, personal discipline alone is never going to make us the self-controlled men we want to be. We need God's power for that. However, while the Holy Spirit does the work in us, he does not do all the work for us. A self-controlled life does demand discipline:

> Do you not know that in a race all the runners compete, but only one receives the prize? So run that you may obtain it. Every athlete exercises self-control in all things. They do it to receive a perishable wreath, but we an imperishable. So I do not run aimlessly; I do not box as one beating the air. But I discipline my body and keep it under control, lest after preaching to others I myself should be disqualified.
>
> (1 Corinthians 9 v 24-27)

The discipline, drive and desire of a gold-medal athlete. The punishing training-regime of a prizefighter. This, and no less than this, is what is required of us if we are going to become men of self-control.

If you want to run a marathon, you start training, and you keep training. It doesn't matter if it's raining, snowing or blowing a hurricane—you train. Likewise, if you want to be self-controlled, you need to start establishing godly habits, and keep going with them. You need to have the discipline to build the walls and battle temptation in all the seasons of your life, every day.

Where do you lack discipline right now?

- Do you need to leave your smartphone charging downstairs in order to eradicate late night procrastination or lust?

- Would a Bible-study plan / prayer guide help you to be more diligent in your devotional life?

- Might it help you to find a dedicated training partner to help you get back in shape?

- Do you need to cut your credit card in half and go cash-only for a while?

Brick #6: Passion

It is likely that, like me, you have tried at various times to gain control over your life by depriving yourself of certain "pleasures". You stop drinking, purge your DVD collection, give up junk food, and so on. In fact, you use all the bricks I've already listed.

These are all good things, but they don't eradicate the baseline desires that make us want to sin. This is because self-control cannot be achieved by the suppression of our passions alone. We are by nature people of passion, created in the image of a passionate God, and he does not want us to be passionless.

He wants to redeem and reconfigure our passions.

When it comes down to it, our lack of self-control is a worship issue. We choose to lust after idols instead of loving God. Therefore what is required is not idol dis-placement, but idol re-placement. Our objective is not to somehow "switch off" our passions, but rather to redirect them towards the One for whom our passion primarily exists. To love him who first loved us. To allow our hearts to burn with hot and holy devotion for the Redeemer, who poured out his passion for us on the cross.

Self-control is about so much more than merely saying "no" to yourself—it's about saying a resounding "yes" to Jesus. That's why just before Paul told the Roman church to "make no provision for the flesh, to gratify its desires", he told them to "put on the Lord Jesus Christ" (Romans 13 v 14).

That's what Jesus was getting at when he said:

> If anyone would come after me, let him deny himself and take up his cross and follow me. For whoever would save his life will lose it, but whoever loses his life for my sake and the gospel's will save it. (Mark 8 v 34-35)

What is required is both "deny yourself" *and* "follow me". It's not just reject sin; it's enjoy Jesus! Going after self-control is about the delight of pursuing a relationship with Jesus, not the drudgery of practising dead religion. We love sin less as we love Jesus more.

With this in mind, here are a few final challenges and questions for you to consider:

- Can you identify the idols that lurk behind your three target areas of weakness?
- What is it they seem to offer that makes them so appealing? In what ways is Jesus better?
- Take some time to repent; to de-throne your idols and to re-throne Jesus as your King.
- What steps can you take to grow deeper in your love for Jesus?

Roll those sleeves up…

You can't build without a blueprint. You have the life of Christ.

You can't build without clearing the wreckage. You have the death of Christ.

You can't build without foundations. You have the word and work of Christ.

You can't build without cement. You have the Spirit of Christ.

It's very hard to build without a gang. You have the church of Christ.

You can't build without bricks. Mercifully, you have been supplied with a shipment of solid bricks with which to build.

But even with all this, *you still have to build*. It's hard work, but it's work that's worth it. You have everything you need to build a life of self-control.

How will you start building towards lasting self-control today?

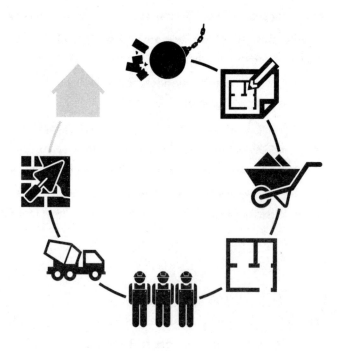

Steve's story

Gluttony is one of my biggest struggles. Looking at me and knowing me many people would not recognise this. I played all different sports growing up, especially football. I'm 6 feet tall and 12 and a half stone. But what people don't see is how often I think about and turn to food for satisfaction, joy and security. I take a good thing and make it a god thing.

So the Lord has helped me use certain disciplines and habits to fight the sin of gluttony and to grow in self-control.

The first thing the Lord did was to make me aware of this sin and show me it's an issue of finding my joy and pleasure in another place other than Jesus. One verse that hit me was Philippians 3 v 19: "Their god is their belly". So the first discipline I exercise regularly is reading my Bible daily. It's how I come to Jesus, the only true "bread of life" (John 6 v 35).

The second discipline is fasting. It's interesting to see that it's one of the first disciplines the New Testament encourages (Matthew 6 v 16-18). I have done monthly fasts or 40-day fasts, just eating one meal a day and drinking plenty of fluid. The goal here is to spend a prolonged period of time using the hours I would use for eating to be with the Lord. This discipline has shown me how much I eat food not to live and survive, but to cover and medicate hurts and dissatisfactions in my life.

Finally exercise is a key part of my life. I try to go jogging three or four times a week. I'm not the fastest of runners and I don't go for the longest of distances! But looking after the body the Lord has given me is important. I use the time to pray, listen to a sermon on my iPod, or think about a Bible passage. And after the hard work of the run, I'm less likely to eat the extra plate of food or grab that packet of crisps!

Bible-reading, fasting, and exercise. These are the three ways I've found to build a habit of self-control in this area. With God's help, it's working.

9. Home

Never, ever, ever, ever, ever give up.

Winston Churchill

Part of my commitment to not becoming a fat pastor is to get out on my mountain bike whenever I can. I am blessed to live in the Welsh valleys, where I can literally open my back gate and ride straight up into the Brecon Beacons range of hills. I love this part of my life... and I also hate it! I hate it because between my back gate and the top of the mountain is a savage uphill track that assaults every muscle in my legs, obliterates my lungs and generally makes me want to die.

But that's kind of why I love it too, because nothing beats the sense of satisfaction I get when, breathless, sweaty and wrecked, I finally make it to the summit. The views from the top are awe-inspiring.

Even so, sometimes it seems too hard. My legs stop pedalling, and I grind to a halt. It's on those occasions that I have to get straight back on the bike. The longer I leave it, the more stiff I'll get and the harder it will be to get going again.

My Christian journey often feels like riding my bike up that track. Sometimes the daily pull of sin feels impossible to conquer. The shame of failure can be too painful to bear, and the relentless onslaught of trials and temptations too much to deal with. Progress can be agonisingly slow and sometimes I lose control.

And on days like that I just want to give up and quit. But I need to get back on the bike, and fast. I have discovered that "quick repentance" is crucial in not losing momentum. I try never to end the day without confessing my sin to Jesus and receiving his forgiveness. That way, I receive grace to continue onwards and upwards.

Building self-control is an uphill struggle. Let's be honest: it is never going to be easy. But the end of our journey is going to be worth it:

> So think clearly and exercise self-control. Look forward to the
> gracious salvation that will come to you when Jesus Christ
> is revealed to the world. So you must live as God's obedient
> children. Don't slip back into your old ways of living to satisfy
> your own desires. You didn't know any better then. But now
> you must be holy in everything you do, just as God who
> chose you is holy.   (1 Peter 1 v 13-15, NLT)

The key to persevering in self-control is to maintain an eternal perspective. Your struggle will soon be over; one day the bliss and beauty of heaven will be your permanent reality. You are headed for a glorious city whose walls can never be breached by sin, suffering or sadness. Until you get there, live like you belong there. Think clearly. Be self-controlled. Don't slip back. Live a godly life. Know you're saved each time you hit the dirt.

One day, you'll be at the top. You'll be able to stop, let down your guard, and breathe in the sweet fragrance of eternal rest. With uninhibited passion, undivided hearts, shameless devotion and inexplicable joy, surrounded by brothers and sisters, you'll declare the excellencies of our mighty King and matchless Saviour, Jesus Christ.

You will be there one day. But until that day, we keep building, brick by brick. Every day, we look at the blueprint, clear the wreckage, lay the foundation, commit to our church, seek the Spirit's help, and get the bricks in place. There's no one's story at the end of this chapter, because it's time to look to your own.

Every day, we build self-control that lasts. For our joy, for the sake of those we love, and for God's glory.

Brick by brick. Till we're home.

Thank you...

... to my wife Michelle for years of love, laughter and missional madness! You inspire me and help me to love Jesus more than you know. I'd be lost without your gracious support and encouragement. You float my boat and rock my world!

... to the Hankey kids, for making family fun. For helping me keep things in perspective. For teaching me stuff about myself and Jesus that you don't even know you're teaching me. You rock my boat and wreck my stuff!

... to Jim and Naomi, Jeff and Jen, for being such a blessing to lead with and serve alongside. Thanks for bearing with me, standing with me, challenging me, and giving me time, space and grace to write books and stuff!

... to the Fight Club boyos, for going toe to toe, and standing shoulder to shoulder, with me. For pushing me, provoking me and helping me to keep putting my flesh to death.

... to the staff at Starbucks in Cwmbran, for not objecting to me pretty much living in your shop for months on end, buying the cheapest coffee possible, taking hours to drink it and rinsing your wifi and free refills!

... to The Good Book Company, not least my legendary editor, Carl Laferton, for believing in this project from the very start. This book is as much down to your hard work and creative input as mine. Thanks so much.

... to Jesus, for saving me, sanctifying me and never giving up on me. I pray this book will help other men to experience the same grace and freedom that has revolutionised my life. If that happens I'll be buzzin', and you'll be glorified!

Other books in the (live) differen† series

Eternity Changes Everything
Stephen Witmer

This book will thrill you with the difference that eternity makes to us right now. It excites us about what life after death is like, and inspires us to live more contented, patient, loving lives today. If you've ever thought heaven should make more of a difference to you, this is a book to read.

"Reading this is like enjoying a coffee with a new friend as he shares the secret of the universe with you."

Jared Wilson, pastor and author of "Gospel Wakefulness"

"This has hugely shifted my outlook. It will change lives. Make sure you read it." *John Hindley, pastor and author of "Serving without Sinking"*

Look out for...

- **Serving without Sinking:** How to serve Christ and keep your joy *by John Hindley*
- **Honest Evangelism:** How to talk about Jesus even when it's tough *by Rico Tice (*out early 2015*)*
- **You Can Really Grow:** How to actually make progress in your Christian life *by John Hindley* (out spring 2015)
- **Time for Everything?** How to be busy without being guilty or crushed *by Matt Fuller* (out summer 2015)

Order from your local Good Book website:

UK & Europe: www.thegoodbook.co.uk • US & Canada: www.thegoodbook.com
Australia: www.thegoodbook.com.au • New Zealand: www.thegoodbook.co.nz

Also by Dai Hankey

THE HARD CORPS

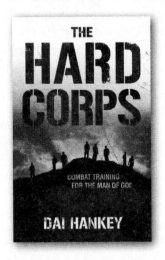

This book brings to life the gripping stories of the Mighty Men who fought alongside King David. Read about the guy who wrestled a lion in a pit on a snowy day... the man who took on an Egyptian twice his size... the three special-ops warriors who risked all in enemy territory just to get a bottle of spring water for their general

But these are not just bed-time tales of heroic men. They are stories that shine a powerful and sometimes uncomfortable light on what it means for you to live as a true man of God—a Christian—today.

> "Pick up *The Hard Corps* and let the Spirit of God encourage and challenge you."
>
> *Matt Chandler, President of Acts 29*

thegoodbook
COMPANY
Opening up the Bible

At The Good Book Company, we are dedicated to helping Christians and local churches grow. We believe that God's growth process always starts with hearing clearly what he has said to us through his timeless word—the Bible.

Ever since we opened our doors in 1991, we have been striving to produce resources that honour God in the way the Bible is used. We have grown to become an international provider of user-friendly resources to the Christian community, with believers of all backgrounds and denominations using our Bible studies, books, evangelistic resources, DVD-based courses and training events.

We want to equip ordinary Christians to live for Christ day by day, and churches to grow in their knowledge of God, their love for one another, and the effectiveness of their outreach.

Call us for a discussion of your needs or visit one of our local websites for more information on the resources and services we provide.

UK & Europe: www.thegoodbook.co.uk
North America: www.thegoodbook.com
Australia: www.thegoodbook.com.au
New Zealand: www.thegoodbook.co.nz

UK & Europe: 0333 123 0880
North America: 866 244 2165
Australia: (02) 6100 4211
New Zealand (+64) 3 343 1990

www.christianityexplored.org

Our partner site is a great place for those exploring the Christian faith, with a clear explanation of the good news, powerful testimonies and answers to difficult questions.

One life. What's it all about?